"My clients often say, 'We've been through this. Things get better for a week or a month, but then we're right back to where we started.' Many self-help books provide a feel-good experience by giving a quick infusion of empathy. Yes, it's very important to feel that you are not alone. However, this book goes far beyond this, providing tools for lasting change."

Carl G. Hindy, PhD, Coauthor of *If This Is Love, Why Do I Feel So Insecure?*

"*The Post-Traumatic Stress Disorder Relationship* is truly the toolbox the partner of a PTSD sufferer needs if he or she wants to help save the partner, their relationship, and their children from the potentially devastating consequences of this disorder."

Jesse J. Harris, PhD, Colonel, U.S Army Retired, Former Social Work Consultant for the Army Surgeon General; Professor and Dean Emeritus, School of Social Work, University of Maryland, Baltimore; and a Recipient of the National Association of Social Workers Lifetime Achievement Award

"Full of sound information as well as useful case studies and exercises, this book is going to be a welcome road map for the partner who wants to support a loved one with PTSD—a must read."

Colonel Robert I. Miller, MD, Commander of Malcolm Grow Medical Center, Andrews Air Force Base, Maryland

"This is a book overflowing with information, sound advice, and exercises to help you turn what might seem like a tragedy into a springboard for personal and relationship growth."

René J. Robichaux, PhD, LCSW, Colonel, U.S. Army Retired, Former Army Social Work Officer and Chief, Behavioral Health Division, U.S. Army Medical Command

"*The Post-Traumatic Stress Disorder Relationship* should be required reading for everyone who knows someone affected by PTSD. It is a treasure chest of tools that can be used for life to help oneself, their partner, and their children understand and deal with the devastating consequences of PTSD."

Richard Miller, PhD, Clinical Psychologist and Developer of Integrative Restoration (iRest), a program that helps PTSD sufferers heal or better manage PTSD symptoms

"A MUST-READ book for behavioral health professionals, as well as anyone who has, or might have, a partner who is suffering with PTSD. This very well-written book offers vital help and hope to deal with PTSD in relationships—in a most realistic, practical, clear, and immediately applicable manner."

Gregory C. Meyer, D.S.W., Colonel, U.S. Army Retired, Former Social Work Consultant, HQ 7th Medical Command, U.S. Army, Europe

"Dr. Diane England has written a comprehensive book that will answer all of the questions that arise when in a relationship with someone affected by PTSD."

David Riklan, Founder, SelfGrowth.com

"Diane England's book, *The Post-Traumatic Stress Disorder Relationship*, provides extraordinary service to couples who have suffered in silence from this devastating disorder. Now, with Diane's help, couples can fully understand the nature of post-traumatic stress, how it affects their relationship, and what to do about it. If you love someone with post-traumatic stress, get this book and begin following the advice today!"

Nina Atwood, MEd, LPC, Author of *Soul Talk: Powerful, Positive Communication for a Loving Partnership*, and *Temptations of the Single Girl: The Ten Dating Traps You Must Avoid*

The Post-Traumatic Stress Disorder *Relationship*

How to Support Your Partner and Keep Your Relationship Healthy

DIANE ENGLAND, PHD

Avon, Massachusetts

Published by
Adams Media, a division of F+W Media, Inc.
57 Littlefield Street, Avon, MA 02322. U.S.A.
www.adamsmedia.com

ISBN 10: 1-59869-997-0
ISBN 13: 978-1-59869-997-5

Printed in the United States of America.

10 9 8 7 6 5 4 3 2

Library of Congress Cataloging-in-Publication Data
is available from the publisher.

This publication is designed to provide accurate and authoritative information
with regard to the subject matter covered. It is sold with the understanding that
the publisher is not engaged in rendering legal, accounting, or other professional
advice. If legal advice or other expert assistance is required, the services of a competent professional person should be sought.

—From a *Declaration of Principles* jointly adopted by a Committee of the
American Bar Association and a Committee of Publishers and Associations

Many of the designations used by manufacturers and sellers to distinguish their
product are claimed as trademarks. Where those designations appear in this book
and Adams Media was aware of a trademark claim, the designations have been
printed with initial capital letters.

This book is available at quantity discounts for bulk purchases.
For information, please call 1-800-289-0963.

Contents

Acknowledgments   **ix**

Introduction   **xi**

01

1 An Introduction to
PTSD

02

27 Commonly Prescribed
Medications

03

45 Therapeutic
Approaches for PTSD

04

67 Finding the Right
Therapist for Your
Partner

05

85 More Possible Tools
for Your Loved One

06

99 What Are You Going
Through?

07

115 Take Care of Yourself
First

08

133 Change Your Thinking

09

153 Tools for a Better
Relationship

10

183 Coping with Painful
Realities

11

211 Meeting Your
Children's Needs

12

237 Should You Stay?

Afterword **253**
Bibliography **255**
Index **265**

Acknowledgments

A book is never the product of one person's efforts, and so it was with *The Post-Traumatic Stress Disorder Relationship*. I wish to thank my acquisitions editor at Adams Media, Katrina Schroeder, for providing me the opportunity to write a book I could believe in, especially after having worked with so many fine military families at a base in Italy—including during part of the Afghanistan and Iraq Wars. I want to thank my development editor, Katie Corcoran Lytle, who improved the manuscript immensely through reorganization of the content, tightening of my writing, and tweaking of language. I also want to thank Paula Munier, Director of Product Innovation at Adams Media and former President of the New England Mystery Writers of America, for referring me to Katrina. Furthermore, I extend my gratitude to Vaughn Hardacker, a mystery writer and former Marine who fought in Vietnam and understood PTSD's often horrific legacy, for first introducing me to Paula Munier.

I am grateful for the friendship of Gail Hartin, who paved the way for me to work with military families overseas. I appreciated the opportunity to work with Debbie Fabiani, who was first a fellow professional and later a friend who made it possible for me to come to know Italy and some of its people in ways I couldn't have otherwise. I feel blessed to have known someone like Phyllis Marvin, who could just as easily have retired from the Red Cross a few years back, but instead chose to be a grandmother figure for our young military members in Iraq.

I thank Dr. Savan Wilson, who took me into her home in Italy for two months after I suffered what for me was a traumatic event—plus how can I thank all of you who gathered around me regularly during this time? I also appreciated how my boss, Major Marc Silverstein, and my coworkers were there to lend a helping hand, too.

I cannot list everyone here who has made such a difference in my life, but you know who you are. Even if I am terrible about staying in touch, know that you have touched my heart, and often memories of you and good times we once shared have kept me going through the long days of solitude and isolation that writing so often requires. Perhaps once my life is more normal again, we might have the chance to reconnect.

Let me say, though, I especially want to express my love and gratitude to my mother, Sophia Bischoff, who has never ceased to support me or encourage me to go forth and follow my dreams.

Introduction

Are you confused, in emotional pain, and seeking answers because your partner seems distant, lashes out in irritation or anger for no apparent reason, doesn't want to engage in the fun things he or she used to enjoy with you or the family, and appears to have lost any desire for regular sexual activity—all since developing post-traumatic stress disorder, or PTSD? Actually, the situation may be worse than this. Since developing PTSD, your partner may have begun using drugs or alcohol to try to manage the problematic symptoms that arrive with this disorder. But, of course, your partner's substance abuse only creates more problems—or worsens those PTSD symptoms that have been negatively influencing you, your partner, and your relationship.

Perhaps you're involved in a relatively new romantic relationship, but are concerned because some of your partner's behaviors or reactions seem so different from those of previous love interests. Not realizing these may stem from PTSD symptoms associated with a traumatic past, are you blaming yourself unfairly for what is likely the increasingly disappointing quality of this relationship?

If either of these scenarios ring true for you, keep on reading. The content of this book will prove enlightening, providing background information you need about PTSD to better understand its defining symptoms and how these can sculpt your partner into someone you hardly recognize. You'll also come to understand how the presence of PTSD influences you and the relationship the two of you share.

The book also emphasizes the importance of early PTSD treatment through medications and psychotherapy—including those especially recommended for PTSD stemming from combat trauma or sexual assault. You'll also be guided on how to find the best-qualified therapists so that your partner's PTSD isn't allowed to rage on unchecked. Certainly, PTSD left untreated will have a negative impact on you, your partner, and your relationship—especially if your loved one begins to drink heavily to try to manage his or her problematic symptoms. That's why this book, while about your PTSD-impacted relationship, also emphasizes the treatment of the disorder. Just as the couple impacted by alcoholism won't see their relationship improve until the one person's drinking is brought under control, so it will be for you and your partner—the defining symptoms of PTSD must be dealt with first.

Please realize that, just as not all cancer drugs work on all types of cancer, not all therapeutic approaches work for all types of PTSD. If the PTSD stems from war trauma rather than sexual assault, it will need to be treated differently. Also, if the PTSD stems from sexual assault that occurred in a war zone—something some of our fighting men and women have faced—the PTSD case becomes even more complicated. Fortunately, the Department of Veterans Affairs (VA) has responded. They have developed programs that cater to females, who are the majority of such victims.

A Successful Relationship

Because you might be the key to your partner getting appropriate treatment—and staying with it—it's important for you to understand what your partner needs, what's available today that can help even long-term PTSD sufferers, and how to be your partner's advocate in a health care system that can be challenging to navigate. You can help both your partner and your relationship improve by encouraging and supporting your loved one's treatment regimen. But, of course, change won't happen overnight. That's why this book also teaches skills you'll want to use to manage your own thinking and behaviors—in ways that better serve you, your partner, and your relationship. After all, when you know the realities of what you face, are knowledgeable about your options, and strive to move past your fears, you can make conscious choices and create the future you desire rather than reacting to whatever life tosses your way.

By establishing a supportive environment, exhibiting the patience your partner needs to adopt healing behaviors, and being a cheerleader, you can influence whether your partner succeeds in getting rid of those PTSD symptoms—and then successfully manages those that linger. Since this is a daunting task, remember that your loved one's degree of success will ultimately decide the quality of the relationship the two of you come to share. Will that relationship be healthy enough that you can embrace it and remain, or will it become so destructive that you feel compelled to leave?

However, while you need to take actions to help your partner, you must also maintain your own mental health. You'll be guided on how to do this with the worksheets and exercises that you'll find throughout the book. Think of this as a mental exercise program. The benefits you derive from the completion of these worksheets and exercises will depend on the effort you put forth.

It is always important to keep in mind that, while your actions are important, your PTSD-suffering partner must also be willing to seek treatment and actively practice new skills and activities if your relationship is to see significant change. Your partner may fail to realize that PTSD is a predictable reaction on the part of his or her brain to the event of trauma. So, just as it's acceptable to have one's heart treated for an abnormal rhythm, it's common for the brain to need medical treatment to return to normal functioning after exposure to trauma—something your partner needs to understand.

You Need Support Too

This book encourages you to become the supportive partner your loved one needs to move beyond problematic PTSD symptoms, but to help you become that type of partner, you need some support yourself. Do you have a friend or relative who can offer encouragement and be your cheerleader? Perhaps this person can also hold you accountable for doing the exercises this book recommends? In fact, you might want to tell this person how you're trying to put your new knowledge or skills to use, and then describe the changes you're seeing in your relationship as a result. By the way, talk about those baby steps, too. If you wait to describe only significant accomplishments, you'll fail to see how things have slowly been improving for you, your partner, and your relationship—and may become needlessly discouraged. I certainly don't want that to happen!

Take What You Like and Leave the Rest

While you're reading, it's important for you to remember that a book cannot be written to meet the needs of all readers. Therefore, some ideas and exercises set forth may not be relevant to your situation or relationship—at least not today. However, that doesn't mean they are wrong or won't work at a later date. So, take what you like and leave the rest—at least for now. You might want to come back periodically and recheck whether something you previously disregarded might serve you today.

Another word of caution: if you're with someone whose PTSD suddenly arrived and disrupted your life, the part of you that wants things to be as they were before might find reason to ignore much of the information laid out in this book. If this starts to happen, push aside the temptation to slide into denial about what's really happening, and continue to complete the exercises. Remind yourself that things have changed and, as a result, you must too. Practice the behaviors or skills outlined and then take note of how your relationship is beginning to improve. So, are you ready to get started on this new journey?

Chapter 1

An Introduction to PTSD

3   What Is Post-Traumatic Stress Disorder?

4   Who Gets PTSD?

12 PTSD Symptoms

19 Tracking Your Partner's Symptoms

Has your relationship with your loved one taken a nosedive since your partner was diagnosed with PTSD? Do you sometimes wonder if you even have a relationship anymore? But of course you're concerned as you cope with a partner who seems more like a stranger than the person you've always loved. Of course you're concerned when your partner wants to be alone all the time, lashes out at you in anger for no apparent reason, doesn't want to do the fun things that he enjoyed previously, and even wants to avoid sexual contact. Perhaps your partner is unable to hold a steady job, making you the primary breadwinner? If you have children, they may be upset because their once loving parent now seems to be rejecting them. These things certainly all interfere with a loving relationship, and are common in people suffering from PTSD.

Even if you're in a relationship with someone who had PTSD at the time the two of you met, you may be wondering if you can withstand all the problems that this disorder brings. Perhaps you began the relationship with high hopes that, with your support, your partner's PTSD symptoms would somehow dissipate, but are now beginning to realize that this may not be the case. Furthermore, your partner may be using alcohol or drugs as a means to manage his PTSD symptoms. While this is quite common, substance abuse just exacerbates the challenges PTSD brings forth.

Whenever you're facing any one of the numerous problems that PTSD creates, it's helpful to know the truth about what you're dealing with. You stand a better change of managing things effectively this way. Remaining ignorant about the problem—or staying in denial—won't help anyone. When you're knowledgeable, instead of struggling to cope with everything PTSD may be tossing at you day after day, you can begin to take action that will make you feel less helpless—and more hopeful. You'll begin to realize that, while you are not crazy for reacting as you have to this unwelcome guest, there are ways to respond that are better for you, your partner, and your relationship. Also, if you have children, things will be better for them if you and your partner can maintain a less turbulent relationship. Of course, to get to that place where you can be more proactive, you need to understand what PTSD is in the first place.

What Is Post-Traumatic Stress Disorder?

As its name implies, post-traumatic stress disorder is apt to develop after an individual has directly experienced, witnessed, or been confronted with one or more traumatic events. A traumatic event involves some experience that overwhelms the person's ability to cope and compromises her well-being or personal integrity. Often this event involved the actual death of one or more persons, or it evoked intense fear and the belief that death or serious injury to the self or others was imminent.

A brain impacted by trauma reacts by sending a message of danger to the body. The body then slips into survival mode, a fight-or-flight reaction. You've probably experienced this adrenaline-filled reaction at some point during your own life. Your heart rate increased. Your breathing became more rapid as your body prepared to take action. And then, when the threat passed—or the brain reassessed the situation and realized you were not at great risk after all—your heart rhythm and breathing slowed.

When someone develops PTSD, something different happens. It's as if the fight-or-flight reaction never shuts off. As a result, the system of the PTSD sufferer remains aroused, prepared both emotionally and physically to engage in fight or flight. The sufferer typically experiences significant distress or impairment in social, occupational, and other important areas. Needless to say, this is detrimental to the PTSD sufferer's physical body, mental well-being, and relationships with others. PTSD symptoms create havoc in your partner's life and, because the two of you are in a relationship, you can't help but be affected. When one part of a system is malfunctioning—as is the case with your partner because of the PTSD—the entire system will break down. Of course, your partner didn't ask for this to happen. She is initially a helpless victim of the brain's reaction.

Who Gets PTSD?

Not everyone who experiences a traumatic event will develop PTSD. The nature of the person's past and of the trauma itself both appear to play important roles. We now suspect that some people may even be genetically predisposed to developing PTSD. Actually, approximately 8 percent of our population will suffer from this disorder at any point in time. While we are currently hearing about many men and women developing PTSD as the result of being in a war zone, in peacetime the majority of PTSD cases result from motor vehicle accidents. However, your partner may also have developed PTSD from surviving:

- A natural disaster such as a hurricane, tornado, or tsunami
- A house fire or a building collapse

- Rape or another type of sexual assault—which may have occurred in a war zone
- A terrorist attack
- Political imprisonment and torture
- Ongoing domestic violence in a previous relationship
- A carjacking or robbery—likely at gunpoint

Then again, your partner may have developed PTSD after standing by helplessly and watching a family member or loved one be maimed or killed in an accident. We also frequently see PTSD develop in many who experience orthopedic injuries, painful and disfiguring burns, and life-threatening illnesses. Some women even experience PTSD after childbirth.

There are three categories of people most apt to become plagued by the most complicated cases of PTSD. There are adults with painful childhood histories who then experience trauma in adulthood, sexual assault survivors, and war veterans. These sufferers are more likely to not only encounter severe PTSD symptoms but also to develop additional mental health issues such as alcohol or substance abuse problems, depression, or other forms of anxiety.

Victims of Childhood Trauma

Children who are abused physically or sexually, neglected, or abandoned in early childhood either develop PTSD at a very young age or are more likely than the average person to develop PTSD in adulthood after experiencing any form of trauma. Again, these individuals are also apt to experience more severe cases of this disorder. This is partly because an individual who has had a traumatic past is inclined to step into adulthood and engage in behaviors that can lead to even more trauma. For example, to try to cope with the emotional pain of that childhood trauma, the individual might begin abusing drugs. In order to obtain the drugs, he may become involved in situations or with individuals that put him at risk of becoming abused or harmed—or of watching this happen to another. As a result, this individual becomes further traumatized.

Sexual Assault Survivors

Sexual assault is defined as any type of sexual activity involving one or more people who force another to engage in one or more sexual acts or behaviors against his or her will. Rape is a common form of sexual assault, but sexual assault is not limited to actual intercourse. Not only can both men and women become the victims of sexual assault, but either sex can be so profoundly affected by it that both may develop PTSD as a result. However, since more women are sexual assault victims than men, let's talk specifically about this group.

Most women who experience sexual assault in adulthood are assaulted by men they already know—a husband, a former husband, a boyfriend, or a former boyfriend—not perfect strangers. Furthermore, many of these women were the victims of childhood physical or sexual abuse. Why is this so? Often, women who were abused by people they knew and trusted as children find themselves attracted to abusive individuals; they feel chemistry with these men and find the nice guys boring. In fact, these women may have come to equate sex with danger. To feel anything or to be orgasmic, they've discovered that they have to place themselves in situations where sexual assault also is more likely to happen. Also, because of their childhood experiences, they typically don't have a good sense of what is normal behavior and what is not. They may not see the red flags that women from healthier backgrounds would spot instantly. Furthermore, because these women were often abused by the very people who should have had their well-being at heart, they didn't learn how to develop good personal boundaries.

Women with such histories often have trouble saying no to men's sexual advances, no matter how distasteful they may be. Furthermore, these women are easily manipulated by men intent upon treating them as sex objects—there to be used to fulfill desires and fantasies, no matter how hurtful or degrading these may be for the woman. Afterward, these women may come to believe that they engaged in consensual sexual acts when, indeed, they were essentially convinced to believe this by their abusive partners.

Some women with childhood sexual assault histories are also driven at an unconscious level to recreate the type of abuse they experienced as children—expecting to maintain control over the situation this time and to rectify the wrongs of the past. However, not only is it impossible to change something that has already occurred, but rather than remaining in control of these sexual encounters, these women are apt to become the victims of others, experiencing sexual assault that leads to PTSD.

Perhaps it shouldn't be surprising that PTSD can arise from sexual assault. It causes harm to the spirit or the inner core of a person—a soul wound—because not only is the body assaulted, but the victim's worldview is as well. The majority of us have a worldview that lets us believe that the world is a safe place, and that it's possible to trust others. We expect people to treat others as they would like to be treated. For assault victims, this foundation for their personal experience of the self is essentially destroyed. They begin to feel that something is missing. There is a sense of emptiness, that they then try to fill with chemical substances, food, risky sexual behavior, or other compulsive behaviors. So, while many sexual assault victims avoid sex after experiencing sexual assault, others begin to engage in risky sexual behavior. Not surprisingly, such behavior sets these women up to experience further sexual assault.

If your partner has recently experienced sexual assault, you should help ensure that she receives counseling so this potentially destructive path is never traveled—or quickly curtailed if she's walking it already. You may want to seek counseling for yourself if you're finding it challenging to deal with your partner's sexual rejection or chronic infidelity, for example. By coming to understand why such behaviors have been transpiring, you may reach a place where you can forgive. When there, you can strive to rebuild the damaged relationship.

Military Sexual Trauma Survivors

Unfortunately, military sexual trauma, or MST, often affects troops both in and outside of the war zone. While both men and women have experienced MST, women—who often know their attackers—are victimized more frequently. The perpetrators of this crime can be others in their units with whom these women work side by side. But they have also been supervisors or higher-ranking individuals who make decisions concerning whether these women will be promoted, or what duty assignments they'll be given. Because of the power that attackers often hold, many of those who experience MST are left feeling helpless and afraid of revictimization by the same perpetrators.

Because great value is placed on unit cohesion in the military—particularly true in a war zone—victims of MST often are reluctant to come forward and take action against their attackers. The military has recently implemented a system whereby sexual assault victims can seek medical and psychological care without reporting to law enforcement, but many victims still won't seek psychological services, fearing repercussions at the hands of the perpetrator as well as harassment from those in their unit.

MST is particularly traumatic because victims not only feel betrayed by people they thought they could trust, but also feel let down by the entire military system—which makes sense when you realize the culture of family the military has traditionally espoused. Furthermore, many of the young people attracted to our voluntary military look forward to being in this type of organizational culture because they grew up in dysfunctional homes where they didn't have the family structure they longed for. This makes this betrayal by colleagues or superiors even more difficult to bear.

Many victims feel further betrayed when they're shunned by their units or commanders when they try to take action through the military channels set in place to deal with such events. For those already struggling with abandonment issues, to be shunned in this way can be particularly devastating. The victim is apt to experience feelings of helplessness, hopelessness, guilt, shame, and other overwhelming emotions that have lingered from childhood. Faced with such overwhelming feelings, the sexual assault victim may well become suicidal. She is looking for a way to end her emotional pain that, in her present changed state of mind, she believes will be everlasting.

If you find yourself dealing with a suicidal partner, it's important to realize that a person is moved to think or actually engage in suicide as a means of escaping this pain, not because the individual truly desires to die. Because suicide and its prevention are necessary to discuss when talking about all individuals with PTSD, not just MST, this topic is further discussed in Chapter 10.

War Veterans

Most of us like to believe that we'll always be led by our own well-defined moral compass. Those who have been in war—or "warriors," as the military may refer to them—have lost this sense of innocence or naiveté. They have seen firsthand that war is hell, and they know that soldiers do things they never believed they could possibly do, things that go against the kind of personal values and morals that may have led them to serve their country in the first place. But these soldiers became capable of doing such things because the military trained them to disregard their moral compasses. They were encouraged to adopt the mantra that you either kill or you'll get killed. Many realize later—sometimes months after they return home—that they're being plagued by flashbacks or nightmares filled with the faces of those they killed.

Because of the nature of their trauma, these veterans will suffer more symptoms than most PTSD sufferers and may come to experience soul wounds. Dr. Edward Tick and Dr. Jonathan Shay, who have both been treating Vietnam War veterans for decades, strongly believe that soul wounds should be seen as an aspect of PTSD stemming from combat. They have heard many veterans speak with great emotional pain about how they felt their souls or fundamental selves slip away after killing someone for the first time. Drs. Tick and Shay also believe that, if these veterans don't take action to bring their souls back, many will suffer an identity crisis so painful that it could lead to suicide.

Perhaps you are seeing something akin to this in your own partner? While this is undoubtedly frightening for both of you, understand that the soul's drive is to create and preserve life. War is the antithesis of this. If your loved one marched forth into a war zone, he likely did so propelled beyond fear by the idea of doing something for a higher good—perhaps not only for the country, but for other people of this world, too. But once beyond the fury of battle, the people that he killed may no longer be seen as the enemy, but merely as people who were trying to defend their homes, families, and homeland. Now perceiving those killed as sharing his humanness, the agony of the veteran begins. Furthermore, your partner may be plagued by something called survivor's guilt—for living through the horrors of war when buddies did not.

Dr. Tick suggests that these PTSD symptoms are there to awaken the veteran to the need to deal with what he has done—how it has impacted his spirit or soul. Many a war veteran returns to the civilian world with no real sense of who he is after breaking a personal ethical code. He is trapped in the emotional pain of a moral dilemma that seems irresolvable. Therefore, for true healing to occur, the veteran must confront painful questions. He must be able to tell highly personal stories saturated with raw emotion—emotion he has very likely been struggling to squelch instead. However, this emotion must be allowed to surface for the combat veteran to be healed. But because he believes this could prove emotionally overwhelming, he may turn to alcohol and drugs to keep the feelings at bay, ultimately exacerbating his problems.

If you're the partner of a war veteran, perhaps by the time you finish reading this book, you'll feel capable of hearing these stories. But even if you can't, you must try to help your partner engage in deeds that are creative rather than destructive—so your partner can come to realize that his soul is still there. Through this realization, your partner should discover profound healing.

PTSD Symptoms

Psychiatrists have determined that PTSD should only be diagnosed after a month has elapsed since the time of the trauma. Prior to then, the person may be labeled as suffering from post-traumatic stress, but not actual post-traumatic stress disorder. Furthermore, the sufferer must exhibit three categories of symptoms that define or distinguish PTSD from other mental health issues. One category of symptoms causes the sufferer to re-experience the traumatic event through nightmares or flashbacks. A second group involves avoidance, where the PTSD sufferer wants to stay away from anything that may remind her of the trauma—and this includes sights, smells, and sounds. She may also exhibit a general lack of responsiveness to all life circumstances. The third group of symptoms centers on hyperarousal. These often result in the PTSD sufferer being irritable all the time or unable to sleep. While these three categories of symptoms are often present immediately following the traumatic event, sometimes they don't show up until much later—resulting in delayed-onset PTSD.

Re-Experiencing Symptoms

This category of symptoms tends to be most problematic for the majority of PTSD sufferers, and for war veterans in particular. Re-experiencing symptoms include recurring nightmares, being bothered by distressing thoughts about the event, experiencing strong feelings of distress, displaying physiological responsiveness such as a surge in heart rate or sweating, and having flashbacks, where the sufferer thinks the former traumatic event is unfolding in the present.

Flashbacks tend to be the most troubling of re-experiencing symptoms for PTSD sufferers. Your partner may not want to do things with you anymore because she doesn't want to risk a flashback occurring in public. You may have been taking this as personal rejection, but think of it as the PTSD talking, rather than your partner. Remind yourself that you have no sense of the horror your partner feels in the midst of a flashback.

———————— CASE STUDY ————————

Brian and Jackie

A war veteran, Brian, recently returned home from Iraq and is now suffering from PTSD. He is in the kitchen talking to his wife, Jackie, when there is suddenly a loud clap of thunder. To Jackie's surprise, Brian jumps on top of her and pushes her to the ground. Jackie struggles to get up, but Brian shouts at her to remain still. Jackie can't breathe and, although she continues to struggle, Brian tries to keep her still.

This may seem like strange behavior unless you know that, while walking in a city in Iraq with his buddies, Brian spotted an insurgent about to throw an improvised explosive device (IED) toward their group. One soldier was walking ahead and didn't realize what was about to happen. Brian jumped on top of his buddy, and pulled him away from where he anticipated the IED would land, saving his friend's life. Sadly, one of his best buddies didn't get out of range of this device and was killed as a result.

Indeed, this event was stored in Brain's memory bank with all the gory details attached—every object he had seen, every sound he had heard, every smell that had infiltrated his nostrils, and every sensation his body had experienced. Brian's brain also stored his feelings of horror at this time. Because the emotion aroused in Brian as this traumatic event unfolded was so strong, it became a memory that would stay with him—and come to haunt him as a flashback.

When Brian heard the clap of thunder, these memories were triggered because—in his mind—this sound was associated with the memory of the exploding IED. Subsequently, all of those stored memories combined and were triggered to form an overwhelming flashback—and Brian believed he was actually back in Iraq. He jumped on his wife, Jackie, as though she were his buddy in the war zone—the one whose life he had tried to save.

A flashback can be triggered by anything, even something that your partner may never suspect because she doesn't consciously remember all the sights, sounds, smells, and things experienced at the time of the traumatic event—even though her brain does. To help you develop more empathy for what your partner is going through, think about the worst thing that has ever happened to you in your life, even if it was more embarrassing than traumatic. Would you like to be forced to relive that event over and over—as if it were actually taking place in the present? Probably not. But your loved one's brain, impacted as it is by PTSD, will force her to have this experience.

Avoidance Symptoms

We've already mentioned how your partner may avoid people and places that are reminiscent of the traumatic event. In addition, even though you may want to talk about what happened, and it could prove helpful for your partner to do so, he will likely want to avoid such a discussion. While these are recognizable symptoms of avoidance, your partner may display other avoidance symptoms you wouldn't consider as such. Having difficulty remembering important parts of the traumatic event, feeling distant from others, feeling as if one's life might be cut short, and having difficulty experiencing positive feelings such as happiness or love fit into this category, too.

In actuality, because of PTSD, your partner likely feels little more than a numbing emptiness. Because of this emptiness, your loved one's loss of interest in previously enjoyed activities may play out in the bedroom as well. Your partner may suddenly show little interest in sex. In men, this numbness can also result in erectile difficulties, which could be another reason he wants to avoid sex. Then, because he wants to avoid sex, he may avoid showing any affection that he thinks may lead you to want or expect sex.

An afflicted man may avoid sex with his partner. However, he may go off and try to become sexually involved with other women, which can, of course, be very emotionally painful for the ignored woman. If you've encountered this difficult reality, remind yourself that it's the PTSD talking—it's not really about you.

If your loved one is feeling numb, it isn't surprising that he doesn't experience the same feelings of love and sexual attraction that he once did, or, if he is a new partner, as other men have shown you. However, because he's quite aware of his previous feelings, and likely anticipated that he would still feel the same way as before, this is undoubtedly both upsetting and embarrassing for him. Your partner may pursue other women not because he has truly fallen out of love with you, but to see if he can even experience such feelings again. He may not accept that he is experiencing sexual numbness because of the PTSD—especially if he wants to deny that he has this disorder in the first place.

Other examples of avoidance include:

- A war veteran may refuse to go to war movies or watch television shows about war. For example, a PTSD-suffering World War II veteran who'd been at the Battle of the Bulge refuses to watch anything dealing with war. He claims it's quite enough to have lived through its horrors.
- A woman raped while staying in a hotel may refuse to stay alone in one again.
- A veteran of the Iraq War may refuse to go to the beach—though prior to his war experience, he liked both surf and sand.
- A survivor of a plane crash may refuse to fly.
- A war veteran who wants to avoid loud crowds may refuse to go to concerts, sporting events, and other things he used to enjoy.

- A rape victim may seek to avoid sex, and may gain a large amount of weight so men won't find her sexually attractive.
- A PTSD sufferer may refuse a more challenging, better-paying job because it involves being around too many people. He may select something less prestigious so he can work outdoors alone instead.

War Buddies

If you're in a relationship with a veteran suffering from PTSD—whether this person is a recent vet or has been one for some years—you may find it upsetting that your partner often wants to be with war buddies instead of you. Try not to take it personally. Realize that what these individuals went through together has resulted in something known as traumatic bonding. This group of veterans likely feel that they have a unique connection because of the way they depended on each other to stay alive. If it makes you feel better, realize that while they may share this special bond, probably all they can talk about together is war.

Even if you wish your loved one would discuss these war experiences with you instead, don't push him to do so. After your partner has learned how to better manage the PTSD symptoms, perhaps the two of you can have such a conversation. However, especially in the case of combat trauma, your partner may never want to talk about it with you because you're a civilian. Your loved one knows that you can't possibly understand what he has been through—and the truth is, you can't. Your partner may also fear that you'll offer harsh judgment if you hear all that he was forced to do in the war zone. You may argue that you won't say anything or become judgmental, but the odds are your body language will give you away. Furthermore, once having heard these things, you may find it challenging to reconcile that the person you've adored could ever do such things.

Your partner doesn't want to take such a risk, especially when he is already having a difficult time reconciling personal wartime actions with the self-image he embraced prior to becoming warfare's victim. Also, he undoubtedly avoids talking about these events because of the fear of triggering a flashback. So, accept the fact that for you, your partner's war stories might have to remain half written. If this hurts you—because you no longer feel a part of his life while his war buddies are—remind yourself that no one person can typically meet all the needs of another anyway. By reminding yourself of this fact, you may find it easier to keep from getting so upset.

Hyperarousal Symptoms

Is your partner always on the alert—on the lookout for danger? A war veteran may insist on walking the perimeter of the house before going to bed, after already checking to see if every door and window is securely locked. However, if you're the partner of a war veteran, you may be dealing with even more than his extreme security consciousness. Is he more controlling since returning from war? Such behavior can be difficult to tolerate normally, but especially if you competently kept the home fires burning while your partner was gone. These behaviors—along with irritability, outbursts of anger, difficulty concentrating, being jumpy or easily startled, and having a difficult time falling or staying asleep—are symptoms of hyperarousal.

Remind yourself that this behavior is a symptom of PTSD. Your veteran may try to restrict your and your children's activities because of his fear that danger lurks around every corner. This isn't going to be easy on any of you, but instead of getting annoyed, remind yourself that as your partner gets treatment, some of these behaviors should also begin to disappear. You may also want to maintain a sense of humor about the situation. Once you have yourself in this frame of mind, you could respond to your partner's attempt to control by saying something like, "It's nice to know you care enough to worry so much about me. However, while you were gone, I embraced my inner warrior and now I think I'm invincible. While it might not be the truth, could you humor me and play along?"

But what if your partner engages in angry outbursts that erupt into violence? You have to realize that just because your loved one wouldn't hurt you before, this may not be true now. Your safety—and that of your children—could someday be at stake. This is one of those topics that you may not want to think about but must, and we'll address it in detail later on in Chapter 10.

Tracking Your Partner's Symptoms

Now that you know about PTSD symptoms, you may want to track those that are plaguing your partner. This isn't to say you must write all of them down as they occur, but cite several examples of the most severe symptoms for each category. As time goes by, continue to cite a few more to demonstrate that they indeed persist. If your partner has entered treatment, track them to see if they are less frequent and severe.

"Why should I do this?" you may be silently thinking. "How is this going to benefit the relationship?" Well, if your loved one is refusing to accept and face PTSD's presence, it may be easier to convince her to get treatment if you can bring forth this type of evidence. Also, when your loved one realizes and seeks help for these symptoms, it's likely that she will get the right type of treatment—and more rapidly—if you can provide health care providers with this type of data up front. Remember, the sooner these PTSD symptoms are minimized, the better things will be for you, your partner, and your relationship.

When the two of you meet with a therapist, you'll be able to pinpoint problematic behaviors and cite examples rather than just making general statements such as "My wife never wants to do anything with the kids and me anymore" or "When my wife doesn't want to do something with me, she doesn't merely tell me she won't do it, but she verbally attacks me." By citing specific examples of what she has done, you'll help open your partner's eyes to changes she can make as opposed to just leaving her hurt and frustrated. The therapist will also swiftly gain insight into the types of PTSD symptoms your partner experiences so that a treatment plan can be devised quickly, avoiding the frustration and wasted time of trial and error. Then you can figure out strategies to deal with these so you don't create more stress for your partner, thereby exacerbating the PTSD symptoms.

Both your partner and you will have some baseline data. Thus, as she receives treatment, you will be able to tell quickly if the approach seems to be working or if another should be tried instead. Also, you can spot changes or improvements—small as these might be—that should help provide both of you with the motivation to continue on this pathway to change.

The examples you've collected could provide an opening for a personal dialogue with your partner. You could say, "I've noticed that you've been engaging in these types of behaviors because of these types of PTSD symptoms. How does it feel to be the person you are today versus the person you were before PTSD stepped in? I can't help but figure it must be tough. Do you want to talk about it?" And then, of course, sit there and listen without judgment to try to rebuild some of the connection you've lost as a couple.

If your loved one developed PTSD as the result of being in the war zone and is having difficulty convincing either the Department of Defense (DOD) or the Department of Veterans Affairs (VA) that this is the case, this data could be vital. If it is on your partner's record that she suffers from an adjustment disorder or personality disorder instead of PTSD, this could keep your loved one from ever receiving health care and other benefits that most war veterans are entitled to. So, you'll want to use this data to fight for the diagnosis of PTSD.

If you and your partner decide to advocate for a change in the stated diagnosis, don't do it alone. Instead, seek legal advice from a civilian attorney. If your partner has PTSD due to service in the Iraq or Afghanistan War, you can seek out the help of Lawyers Serving Warriors for free legal advice. Visit their website at *www.lawyersservingwarriors.com*.

There may be another use for this data that you don't want to consider right now. But if your PTSD-suffering spouse refuses to get treatment, your relationship may deteriorate to a point where it becomes unsafe or emotionally damaging for you or your children to remain with her. In this case your divorce attorney may find this data helpful.

EXERCISE COLLECTING DATA

To ensure this data can be used by others legally, you must attend to how you collect it in the first place. By the way, do *not* consider this or anything else in this book legal advice; seek that out on your own. Again, if your partner is fighting for benefits for a PTSD-related disability, contact Lawyers Serving Warriors earlier rather than later. They like to become involved in the process early on. Now, here are guidelines for PTSD symptom data collection:

- Since this data could end up being used for legal purposes, record it in its own document or notebook to ensure that it's admissible as evidence and won't be tossed out. Do *not* collect this data in a diary, for example, where you track everything else about your life. Also, do *not* write down any of these behaviors on your calendar, scribbling them among your social or business engagements. This will not be acceptable evidence, even if it is true.
- Realize that you must be as objective as possible, which means that you must state only the facts of what was said or transpired. You *must not* contaminate the facts with your thoughts or feelings at the time.
- Consider having a notebook with four separate data-collection sheets. One should be for examples of re-experiencing symptoms. The second should be for avoidance symptoms. The third should be for hyperarousal symptoms. The ➤

fourth should be for other behavioral changes you have observed, assuming that this is a long-term relationship. These last changes might be due to such things as depression, substance abuse, or other forms of anxiety besides PTSD. There is no need for you to try to make a diagnosis. On this page as well as the others, just stick to the facts.

- Realize that while you don't have to record every incident that represents changed behavior stemming from the PTSD, if your loved one is fighting for a changed diagnosis or benefits based upon the diagnosis of PTSD, the more such specific or concrete data you can provide, the better.

- Always include the date and approximate time of the incident where you observed the changed behavior, a brief synopsis of the scene or circumstances, as well as identifying information on any other individuals involved in the incident.

- If one of your partner's main PTSD symptoms is irritability, you may decide to track this on a calendar daily. However, include this calendar in your notebook—along with the other four pages. Determine an irritability scale you'll use on an ongoing basis. A scale of one to ten should work. A ten could indicate your partner was essentially in a rage, whereas a one could mean he was as calm as a cucumber. Before you go to bed each night—provided you didn't fight with your partner right before bedtime—list your loved one's score on the calendar.

- An incident might demonstrate more than one type of PTSD symptom. In this case, you ➤

might type it up on the computer, and then print out two copies of the document. If the incident demonstrates hyperarousal as well as avoidance, file a copy under each symptom category. ∎

CASE STUDY

Sarah and Trent

Sarah, the wife of PTSD sufferer Trent, decides to record an incident that shows her husband's tendency to avoid situations he was comfortable with previously. She also documents a hyperarousal symptom—Trent's tendency to get irritated easily. Sarah uses a notebook she bought for this purpose only, and files the following documentation under both the Avoidance and Hyperarousal Symptoms categories. Here is what she wrote on that page:

Date: Morning of September 1, 2008
Setting: Den in our house—just Trent and I present
Incident Revolves Around: Asking Trent that morning if he wanted to attend the fair with me and the children that afternoon. This is something he always did in years past, or before he was deployed by the Army to Iraq.

Me: *Would you like to go to the fair this afternoon with me and the children? We plan to take off about one o'clock and return by dinnertime.*

Trent: *You know since I got back from Iraq, I hate being in crowds. What in the hell is wrong with you? I have an excuse for my hearing loss. What's yours?*

Me: *I'm sorry. I was thinking about how you enjoyed it in the past, and I completely forgot about that.*

Trent: *Do you realize I could have gotten my buddies killed if I acted the way you do most of the time? Just get out of here and leave me alone.*

I didn't say anything further. I gathered up the children, and we left earlier than planned. When we returned about six hours later, Trent was sitting in the recliner in the den watching a movie—a comedy. He turned the movie off, asked the kids how the fair was, and smiled as they shared their stories. While he was calm at this point, I give him an Irritability Rating of 6 for the day because of the earlier incident— because of how loudly he shouted and the abusiveness of his words.

Since early treatment is so important to impacting this disorder, it's an important thing to know about. This isn't to say that if you are with a longtime PTSD sufferer, he can't be helped; he probably can. So, read on to learn more about treatment. And since symptoms can often be helped with medications, let's start there.

Chapter 2

Commonly Prescribed Medications

29 Drugs Don't Work the Same for Everyone

30 Drug Tolerance

31 Drug Interactions

32 Selective Serotonin Reuptake Inhibitors

39 Treating Rage

40 Medications to Beware Of

43 Illegal Drugs

When your partner has PTSD, everyone and everything suffers. Your partner suffers from those troublesome PTSD symptoms. You likely suffer because you have to watch him suffer. And, of course, your relationship suffers because your partner is essentially incapable of being a partner any longer. But wouldn't your relationship improve if those symptoms, such as your soldier's propensity to rage, suddenly disappeared? And wouldn't it be nice if your partner wasn't fearful of being sexual because medication had alleviated his erection problem? One of the best ways for both of you to find relief is by getting your partner on medications that can help to minimize—or completely alleviate—PTSD symptoms.

While your partner will undoubtedly need psychotherapy, whether this is a new case of PTSD or a long-standing one, it is a good idea to start with the medications. When these have gotten the PTSD symptoms under better control, it will be easier for your loved one to benefit from the techniques or skills learned in psychotherapy. But in truth, these skills may end up having the most profound effect on your relationship.

Before we get into a heavy discussion about medications, it is important to point out that the experts on what are called psychotropic medications—the kind of drugs used to treat mental disorders including PTSD—are often psychiatrists who also hold a PhD in pharmacology. This means they are both medical doctors who specialize in mental disorders and scientists who study the changes produced by chemical substances, especially the actions of drugs used to treat disease. For that reason, much of the information in this chapter is based primarily on information from Stephen Lindley, MD, PhD, from the National Center for PTSD, and Jonathan Shay, MD, PhD, who has served as a staff psychiatrist at the Boston Veterans Administration Outpatient Clinic.

Drugs Don't Work the Same for Everyone

Has your partner already been diagnosed with PTSD and perhaps other mental health issues as well? If so, she may already be taking medications to help minimize problematic PTSD symptoms. But are you still waiting to see some changes related to the medications? Are you wondering if they will work as well for your partner as studies suggest they should?

It is important to realize that not all people respond the same to any given medication. Even if a drug is supposed to effectively treat PTSD, that doesn't mean it will work on every PTSD sufferer. Research studies basically show how a drug performed on a selected group of people. If the drug helped minimize PTSD symptoms in a majority of the subjects in the study, the study will suggest that this drug is effective for treating PTSD. After multiple studies give the same results, the Federal Drug Administration (FDA) will declare the drug effective for tackling PTSD. However, that doesn't mean the approved drug worked well for all people in all the research groups; some may actually have suffered miserable side effects while not experiencing great results.

Also, be aware that the psychiatrist may need to try various dosages of a drug on your partner before he discovers one that really works. After all, while a certain dosage might be recommended because it worked well for most people in the research studies, this same dosage won't necessarily work for your loved one. The recommended dosage might be too high and could cause side effects that seem unbearable. However, these side effects could disappear at a lower dosage, allowing your partner to enjoy the medication's benefits. On the other hand, she may not benefit from the dosage change and, instead, an entirely new medication will have to be tried.

There is a real downside to trying various medications or dosages. After all, with many medications used to treat people with PTSD, a drug's main effect or its benefits could take weeks to kick in. Meanwhile, the drug may have unpleasant side effects that show up immediately, such as jitteriness. If the psychiatrist is forced to prescribe a different drug, your loved one may have to go through several more weeks without getting relief from her PTSD symptoms, which can be very difficult for both of you. Needless to say, your relationship will suffer as long as your partner suffers—a disappointment when you had hoped the drug would quickly change your loved one back to the person you knew before PTSD.

Drug Tolerance

Another potential difficulty is that your partner could build up a tolerance to a helpful drug. Unfortunately, even though a drug works well at a certain dosage for her at first, it doesn't mean it will necessarily work well forever. If her body gets used to a particular medicine, the drug will then stop working as it once did. Either the dosage must be increased to jump-start the drug's effectiveness or your partner will have to switch to a new drug to get the same type of benefit.

Your partner needs to realize that if she must change from one medication to another because of a tolerance to that medication, it might not be possible to switch from one drug to the other quickly. It may be necessary to taper down the first drug's dosage to avoid unsafe withdrawal symptoms. So, encourage your partner to carefully follow medication directions—both those from the psychiatrist and those on the medication's instruction sheet. The consequences of not doing so could be deadly.

Drug Interactions

When a person is taking several different drugs, there's always the chance they could interact and create serious health issues—if not death. In recent times, soldiers who were not assumed to be suicidal have died in their sleep. It is possible these deaths were due to accidental drug overdoses or lethal drug interactions.

Because of this deadly risk, you'll want to pay special attention to your partner's reactions whenever he is given a new drug, or even if a dosage is increased. Also, realize that dangerous drug interactions don't develop solely from mixing prescription drugs; mixing over-the-counter medications with prescription drugs can be equally dangerous. When your loved one initially sees the psychiatrist, it's important to list absolutely everything he is using, as well as the dosages. Then, once your partner is on various medications for the PTSD, don't assume adding any type of medication is safe without clearance from the psychiatrist.

Because your partner can be helped immensely by medications, he should not avoid taking them because of the risks just discussed. Again, he just needs to take them with care. That said, let's look at the medications your loved one is apt to be given.

Selective Serotonin Reuptake Inhibitors

Your partner's symptoms will undoubtedly be treated with something called a selective serotonin reuptake inhibitor (SSRI). Drugs in this class are typically the first line of treatment for PTSD because they help alleviate all three categories of PTSD symptoms instead of impacting only one group. Interestingly enough, they were initially developed and approved by the FDA to treat depression.

Research can't tell us conclusively why the SSRIs work for depression or PTSD, but it appears that when a person suffers from either, there is too low a level of serotonin—a chemical or neurotransmitter that carries messages from one brain cell or neuron to the next. The neurotransmitter takes the message across a gap between the two cells, and it delivers it into a synapse designed exclusively for that neurotransmitter. When the individual takes an SSRI, the serotonin level in the neuron receiving the message becomes higher than it would have been without the medication.

Apparently, this occurs because once the serotonin arrives at the synapse, some of it is typically reabsorbed by the neuron that sent the message, which appears to do nothing to promote brain functioning. However, when the SSRI blocks this reuptake of serotonin, there is then more serotonin available to transport messages to the next neuron. Furthermore, serotonin seems to promote a process called neurogenesis—the growth of new brain cells. It may actually be the increased serotonin level creating growth of new neurons that helps improve the person's mood.

The first SSRI that came to market was *Prozac*, which is generically called fluoxetine. *Prozac* has been on the market for over twenty years. Four other SSRIs have come on the market since that time. The SSRIs are listed below with the generic's name first, followed by the trade name in parentheses.

- Citalopram (*Celexa*)
- Escitalopram (*Lexapro*)
- Fluoxetine (*Prozac*, or *Prozac Weekly*)
- Paroxetine (*Paxil*, or *Paxil CR*)
- Sertraline (*Zoloft*)

The last two SSRIs on this list, paroxetine and sertraline, have been approved by the Food and Drug Administration to treat PTSD. Despite the fact that the other three SSRIs have not been specifically approved for this purpose, they may still be prescribed and work well for the PTSD sufferer. Don't become concerned if your partner's psychiatrist prescribes one of them.

Side Effects

Fortunately, SSRIs tend to lack many bad side effects, and are generally considered the safest class of antidepressants. Why? Because not only are they less likely to have adverse interactions with other medications, but they're also less dangerous if the person overdoses on the drug. Since all SSRIs work in much the same way, you'll see the same side effects listed on all of their information sheets. Nevertheless, each SSRI has some different pharmacological characteristics from the others, which is why your partner may respond differently to one SSRI versus another.

The first dangerous side effect you need to know about is serotonin syndrome, which is uncommon but potentially deadly. Per the Mayo Clinic website, this condition—characterized by dangerously high levels of serotonin in the brain—can occur when an SSRI interacts with a type of antidepressant known as a monoamine oxidase inhibitor (MAOI). Serotonin syndrome might also occur if an SSRI is taken with other medications or supplements affecting serotonin levels—such as *St. John's Wort*. Because serotonin syndrome requires immediate medical treatment, see to it that your loved one gets to an emergency room quickly if he has mixed such medications and suddenly exhibits confusion, restlessness, extreme agitation, fluctuations in blood pressure, increased heart rate, nausea and vomiting, fever, or seizures, or begins to hallucinate. Be sure to tell the doctors what you suspect happened.

Some other common side effects of SSRIs include nausea, headache, diarrhea, nervousness, rash, agitation, restlessness, increased sweating, weight gain, drowsiness, insomnia, and—what may prove particularly upsetting to both you and your partner—sexual problems that may include erectile dysfunction, reduced sexual desire, and difficulty achieving orgasm.

Treating Erectile Dysfunction

Viagra was the first drug approved by the FDA to treat erectile dysfunction. Since then, *Levitra* and *Cialis* have joined *Viagra* on the market. These three drugs all work by relaxing smooth muscle cells. This causes the blood vessels to widen so there is an adequate blood flow to the penis to make an erection possible. However, it's important to keep in mind that while these medications make an erection possible, none of these can make that happen without the man experiencing sexual arousal.

Like SSRIs, these three medications have similar side effects, which include headaches, heartburn, and flushing. In addition, problems can occur when they're mixed with certain types of drugs. For this reason, the FDA advises that a person should not take these medications if he is using alpha-blockers or nitrate medications.

The three drugs differ in how quickly they work, how long the drug remains in the body, and the required dosage. If your partner could benefit from one of these medications, he should talk about the differences in the medications with his physician, and then decide which would be best for him.

Treating Insomnia

Often a PTSD sufferer has trouble getting a good night's sleep because of nightmares, not just because of an SSRI side effect. There may not have been help in the past for many PTSD sufferers who suffered from insomnia, but a drug used for years to lower blood pressure, as well as by men for prostate problems, seems to improve sleep and lessen trauma nightmares. This generic drug is called prazosin, and veterans who've taken it report improved sleep quality, reduced trauma nightmares, a better overall sense of well-being, and an improved ability to function. Interestingly enough, the drug did not affect their blood pressure.

Why does prazosin work? It appears that trauma nightmares arise during light sleep as opposed to during rapid eye movement, or REM, sleep, which usually begins about ninety minutes into the five-stage sleep cycle and is when intense dreaming naturally occurs. Prazosin increases REM sleep because it blocks the brain's response to adrenaline-like neurotransmitters such as norepinephrine, which allows the PTSD sufferer to resume normal dreaming while on the medication.

The sufferer must remain on the medication—otherwise, the nightmares seem to return. Therefore, if your loved one is put on this drug, encourage him to stay on it. Realize that often when people undergoing treatment feel better, they tend to want to give up their medication. They forget that their improvement stems from being on that drug. Your partner might need to be reminded of this. It also might help to remind him that this medication can typically be taken for years without ever needing to increase the dosage.

If your partner is not plagued by nightmares, but just needs some assistance getting a good night's sleep, he may be given not an actual sleeping pill, but the nontoxic antidepressant trazodone. This medication, often sold under the trade name of *Desyrel*, promotes sleep because it has the side effect of promoting drowsiness. While people don't seem to develop a tolerance to this side effect, be aware that your partner may need to take a lower dosage of this drug because he is taking an SSRI. Have him talk to the psychiatrist about this.

Paxil and Pregnancy

Women who take *Paxil* during their first trimester of pregnancy are nearly two times as likely to give birth to a child with a birth defect—in particular, a heart defect—than women who take other antidepressants. As a result, the American College of Obstetricians and Gynecologists suggests that no one use *Paxil* during pregnancy. If your partner is using *Paxil* and wants to, or thinks she might, become pregnant, she should talk to her doctor about switching to another antidepressant or discontinuing treatment with *Paxil*.

She shouldn't stop taking the *Paxil* without contacting her doctor first. She may need to taper off of it for safety reasons.

While SSRIs aren't considered addictive, when a person stops treatment abruptly or misses several doses, it is possible to experience withdrawal-like symptoms, which may include nausea, headache, dizziness, lethargy, or flulike symptoms. This is sometimes referred to as discontinuation syndrome.

Suicidal Feelings

There's still controversy regarding whether SSRIs and other antidepressants can lead to worsening symptoms of depression, increased suicidal thoughts, or even suicidal behavior. Always be on the outlook for these, but especially when your partner is first placed on the medication—or if the dosage is changed. If she experiences such thoughts, talk to the psychiatrist immediately about these symptoms and monitor your loved one closely. She may need to stop the medication if such symptoms worsen.

Returning Soldiers

If your partner is a war veteran with PTSD, you need to realize he may go through a brief period of intense despair during the first few months of being on an SSRI. It may be difficult to see this as improvement, but it actually is. Your partner is moving away from that state of numbness when he felt nothing.

As your partner undergoes this shift from not feeling to experiencing emotions once again, he may begin to realize what he did in the course of war. For example, he may realize he took the lives of innocent women and children although he was a Christian who had long believed "Thou shalt not kill." When he realizes this, he may feel great remorse and, in fact, may come to feel unworthy of your love—because he now sees himself as something akin to a monster. He may also attempt to take his own life, not because the medication made him do it, but perhaps because he became overwhelmed by painful and condemning thoughts that the medication couldn't stop from coming forth.

Please realize that your partner needs to make it through this personal dark night of the soul in order to come out the other side as a man who can put the past behind him, create a new life, and honor the man he wants to become. However, he shouldn't be left alone as he goes through these dark days and nights. He'll need more than medications to get him through this time. He'll need support from other veterans, family members, and at least one therapist he can talk with—not merely a psychiatrist who monitors his medications.

Your wounded soldier may also want to seek out a spiritual guide who can help him realize that while he may have done horrific things in the war zone, there is still a part of him—that inner core—that has essentially remained untouched by those horrors. It is this part of him that he must allow to drive him in the future, so he can move beyond the past. To help him do this, your partner may seek help from a minister, rabbi, or priest who can understand and support him in his effort to use something horrible as the impetus for personal and spiritual growth.

It's important to remember that medications cannot heal the soul wounds of war. Still, when the individual can begin to forgive himself for the evil things he believes himself to have done—as well as to forgive others for what they may have done to him—he is positioned to launch into a new way of living and being. Certainly, you can play an important role in helping to make this happen by ensuring that he has support and is not isolated from others. Also, if you talk to him openly about suicide (we'll discuss how to do this in Chapter 10), and get him to commit to you that he won't kill himself, he'll probably persevere through these tough times.

Treating Rage

An SSRI may also help your partner eliminate detrimental impulsive behavior that is apt to arise when PTSD is present—and this includes explosive anger. Especially with soldiers with PTSD who've been highly trained to react automatically whenever adrenaline starts flowing through their veins, medication is needed to break what Dr. Shay calls the mind-body-mind response. Otherwise, the anger is apt to escalate into rage once the soldier's brain has been triggered to respond in the fight mode.

In Chapter 8, you'll learn techniques that you can use to control any anger you may be experiencing at the changes PTSD has wrought in your partner and your relationship. After all, anyone's brain can be triggered by something that has a familiar pattern, causing that person to overreact to what is happening in the moment. The difference between you and your partner suffering from combat trauma is that you can stop and evaluate whether your response truly makes sense in the moment. Many soldiers cannot do this. While they may want to respond differently, they are unable to do so because military training has changed their brains.

The good news is that these soldiers can be helped with a beta-blocker—a medication typically used to treat high blood pressure. This works for the soldier wounded by PTSD because it interferes with the adrenaline flowing through his body. So, if your combat veteran partner experiences rage attacks, do him, yourself, and your relationship a favor. Talk to the psychiatrist about prescribing a beta-blocker in addition to an SSRI. Even if your partner isn't a war veteran but regularly erupts into rages, talk to the psychiatrist about this option. After all, this medication could help save your partner from experiencing the ongoing humiliation that he likely feels after flying off the handle—behaving inconsistently with the person he knows himself to be at his core. Furthermore, this will help to keep you safer, too.

Medications to Beware Of

While there are helpful medications for PTSD sufferers that typically keep on helping, there are other medications that seem helpful at first, but then create problems down the road. Your partner needs to avoid them because they can create issues such as addiction.

Benzodiazepines

The first family of drugs to watch out for is the benzodiazepines. This family includes:

diazepam, often sold as *Valium*

alprazolam, often sold as *Xanax*

lorazepam, often sold as *Ativan*

triazolam, best known as *Halcion*

Not only are these drugs addictive, but as with alcohol, people lose their inhibitions while using them. When we're sober, there are things we may think about doing or saying, but we control ourselves because we don't want to create trouble or hurt others—especially those we love. But under the influence of alcohol or one of these medications, a person may not only say hurtful things, but she may actually go as far as to commit suicide or murder.

Of course, with PTSD, a person is less aware of the impact of her behavior on others anyway. Therefore, the use of one of these drugs may make an already problematic situation even worse. Benzodiazepines can also cause memory loss. Can you see how problematic or even dangerous it could be if your partner was already having problems thinking clearly and then started taking one of these medications?

Why does the use of benzodiazepines often lead to abuse and addiction? People often believe the drowsy feeling that comes with the use of this drug—a side effect many find pleasant—is its main effect. The person quickly develops a tolerance to the side effect while the drug continues to accomplish what it was designed to do. But having confused the side effect with the main effect of the medication, the person taking the drug may become concerned that her anxiety will soon return. She then increases the dosage to try to get the drowsy feeling again. By doubling up on the medication, however, the PTSD sufferer may be thrust forward on the road to addiction.

Another important fact to know about benzodiazepines is that they quickly enter and leave the body. When a drug leaves the body rapidly, as with *Halcion*, the person can actually experience mini-withdrawals between doses of the drug. In fact, an individual taking *Halcion* might wake up in the middle of the night because of being in the withdrawal phase. Veterans using *Xanax* may experience periods of anxiety and irritability during each day due to mini-withdrawal reactions between doses. But worse yet, some veterans who have been taken off this type of drug after being on it for a long time have engaged in extreme violence.

Can you better appreciate how the benzodiazepines could be bad news for your partner? She should work with the psychiatrist to find another alternative to this family of medications for the treatment of anxiety.

Caffeine

People tend to like caffeine since it often leads to feeling more awake, energetic, and optimistic. What people might be less inclined to realize, however, is that it can have negative psychological effects. In actuality, consuming quantities of caffeine can create anxiety and depression.

PTSD sufferers need to know about problems related to caffeine—which is not just one drug, but three. Each of these three can have a different effect on a person. An individual may do fine with caffeine in its initial state or stage, but after about two hours, the body converts caffeine into theobromine. It stays in this form for about four hours. At that time, the body converts it into theophylline, which lingers in the body for about six hours.

For PTSD sufferers, the problem tends to lie not with the caffeine, but with the other two chemical changes that take place. But because the person may not feel bad until four to six hours after having the caffeine fix, something else that happened during the course of the day—or life in general—may be blamed for causing feelings of depression or anxiety to arise. If your partner slowly removes caffeine from his diet, the depression or anxiety may well disappear.

Illegal Drugs

The person who develops PTSD often gets into situations where he is apt to experience yet more trauma. We see this often with PTSD sufferers who become addicted to street drugs. In order to get the drugs, these individuals become involved in relationships or develop obligations that they wouldn't have without their addictions. They or their loved ones may suffer physical harm at the hands of people who don't share their personal values and who lack any kind of moral compass. Furthermore, this drug lifestyle can result in a great deal of shame, especially for a war veteran who entered the military because he saw it as something honorable. What he came to experience in the war zone may have left him feeling worthless, despicable, and in need of drugs to feel better. However, he'll likely feel worse about himself as he continues to sink further into this lifestyle.

If your partner is not using illegal drugs, he may still try to help out a buddy who is. He may be asked to do dangerous favors such as hold drugs, drug-related weapons, or drug-related money. He may also be called to rescue this friend from a life-threatening situation. Even if things go well, your partner may find himself back in combat mode, instead of striving to remain safe and symptom-free from PTSD.

Of course, if your PTSD-suffering partner is a former addict, it's dangerous for him to hang around users. Former drug addicts or alcoholics are told in twelve-step programs to change their playmates and their playpens. Your partner should make a great effort to abide by this rule if he has this kind of history.

You'll want to support your partner trying to make and sustain these changes. It's going to help you remain safer as well—and will ultimately benefit your relationship. After all, users only have a relationship with their substance of choice. They are not capable of being in a relationship with another person.

If your partner is trying to either get or stay off drugs, alert his psychiatrist. The doctor can likely prescribe a medication to help your loved one accomplish this.

Chapter 3

Therapeutic Approaches for PTSD

46 Your Partner's Advocate

47 What Else Is Your Partner Facing?

48 Protecting Yourself

49 PTSD, SUD, and Depression

52 Treating PTSD on Its Own

55 Eye Movement Desensitization and Reprocessing

62 The Sexual Assault Survivor

The right medications can help your partner. But the right type of psychotherapy will be equally—if not more—important. You need to understand the right type of therapy for your partner, the best treatment for PTSD stemming from combat trauma versus a car accident, for example. Remember, you may encounter therapists who profess to treat PTSD, but aren't up-to-date on treating military sexual trauma (MST), for example, when this is the expertise your partner needs. While you'd expect the therapist to tell you that she is not qualified to treat MST, she may not do so. Therefore, to ensure that your partner ultimately gets the best therapy possible from the most qualified therapist, you need to understand what the right therapy should entail. This chapter will provide that information, and the next chapter will delve into how to find the best therapist to deliver that therapy.

Because the right therapy can be effective, you don't want your partner to become frustrated and give up on therapy early on because she was receiving the wrong kind and not making any progress. Don't risk setting your partner up for the harmful legacy that forsaking therapy will undoubtedly deliver.

Your Partner's Advocate

It is great that you're here to learn about best treatment practices for the various types of PTSD. After all, with all the symptoms your loved one is enduring right now, he probably is not capable of taking on the task of chasing down this information—or of finding a therapist capable of meeting his specific needs. Certainly, taking on this role is both challenging and time consuming; it may be one more task you feel you don't need with everything else you're facing. When you're feeling overwhelmed—which is to be expected, by the way—remind yourself that your goal is to do everything possible to ensure happier and healthier days for you, your partner, and your relationship.

As we embark on talking about therapeutic approaches, it is important to realize there is research currently being done on how to provide better care for the large numbers of war veterans that we expect to see over the next few years. However, many techniques have already been shown to have positive effects on most everyone treated with them. As with medications, they may not prove beneficial to all PTSD sufferers, but the odds are in your loved one's favor. So, here's wishing you the best in your pursuit to help your partner get the best help possible for his or her PTSD.

What Else Is Your Partner Facing?

It's important to face up to everything your partner is dealing with in order to be an effective advocate for him and to help to ensure that he ends up receiving the best help possible. Accept that your partner's PTSD may have brought along unwanted guests such as anxiety, depression, and substance abuse. Acknowledge that these in turn may have led to occupational difficulties or health problems. Of course, all of these have undoubtedly impacted your relationship in negative ways that you'd like to see dealt with as well.

There is a lot to think about. Furthermore, you need to realize that, while it's possible for your partner to take several medications simultaneously to deal with multiple problems, it doesn't work that way with psychotherapy. So, while you may want to work on your relationship, you're not going to get too far if your partner's PTSD symptoms aren't dealt with first—and medication probably hasn't conquered them all. It may be necessary for your partner and the therapist to tackle some of these issues at the same time, but every problem can't be dealt with at once.

Protecting Yourself

You may need to find some way to cope with your partner's irritation and anger until she gets the PTSD symptoms under better control. Of course, you may not want to stick around if your partner's anger grows into rage and gets out of hand, but we'll talk about such things later on in the book. For now, envision yourself in a protective bubble or with some type of a shield that protects you from the hurtful words and other contaminants of your partner's PTSD.

Frankly, your partner could be avoiding you because she doesn't want to harm you with her PTSD-driven behaviors. Remember, your partner realizes that she is a changed person and dislikes this as much as you do. So you might want to assure her that you're not going to let this happen. Tell her that you've got this bubble you're going to wear until she gets into therapy and shows some improvement. Then talk about your commitment to seeing that she gets the best help possible. By taking action, you may start to feel that you have some control over what has probably felt like an out-of-control situation. This should make you feel better. But if this isn't enough, continue to read and do the exercises throughout the book. They—along with the knowledge about the types of PTSD treatment available to your partner—should all help you get through this difficult time.

PTSD, SUD, and Depression

One of the more complex cases of PTSD occurs when your partner also has a combination of substance use disorder (SUD) and depression. If your loved one is abusing alcohol, she may suffer from depression in part because alcohol is a depressant. If this is the case, the depression should lift once your partner goes through detoxification and embraces sobriety. But if she experienced a childhood filled with trauma and remains depressed after obtaining sobriety, realize your partner has likely used alcohol to cope with anxiety or depression stemming from early childhood wounds. As a result, your partner will need a therapist who can treat PTSD, SUD, depression and perhaps anxiety, too.

A person suffering from both PTSD and SUD faces a tougher time of it than a person suffering from either just PTSD or SUD. This person may experience the following challenges:

- While trying to abstain from substance use, painful memories and feelings worsen, which can then cause the PTSD sufferer to relapse.
- The person with PTSD/SUD often won't benefit from the Alcoholics Anonymous (A.A.) Twelve-Step program because A.A. requires the individual to admit that her life has become unmanageable, and that she is powerless over alcohol. However, when the person with PTSD/SUD tries to admit powerlessness, the brain may spot a pattern similar to what happened at the time of the traumatic event, triggering avoidance.
- The PTSD/SUD sufferer may feel like a failure when unable to succeed at treatment programs that others can master. In fact, she may become demoralized and

feel lazy, worthless, bad, and responsible for everything that has happened.

- The symptoms of one disorder may make the sufferer disinclined to take steps to improve the other.
- Some PTSD/SUD sufferers may more readily accept a diagnosis of PTSD rather than SUD. But once the person comes to understand that substances were misused as a form of self-medication—or to block emotional pain stemming from past trauma—it often becomes easier for her to tackle both the SUD and PTSD.
- The sufferer may want to deal with trauma issues early on, but the therapist may disagree. The therapist may not know that research now suggests that simultaneous treatment of SUD and PTSD tends to prevent relapse. Then again, while PTSD, SUD, and other related issues are apt to improve when the two disorders are treated simultaneously, some individuals lack the necessary coping skills and impulse control to engage in such treatment. The therapist may fear the client could experience suicidal thoughts if such treatment is tackled.
- If the PTSD/SUD sufferer wishes to seek help through a therapist who is not associated with a treatment center or community mental health facility, the sufferer may discover that the therapist specializes in either PTSD or SUD, but does not feel equipped to handle the client's needs for simultaneous treatment of both problems.

Seeking Safety

Dr. Lisa Najavits of Harvard University recently developed Seeking Safety, a program helpful for those who have difficulty dealing with simultaneous PTSD/SUD treatment. (You can find out more about this program online at *www.seekingsafety* *.org*. Here, you'll find a manual with session outlines for the therapist as well as handouts for the client.) She realized that PTSD/SUD could be devastating because these disorders may cause the sufferer to lose his personal ideals. For example, many PTSD/SUD sufferers tend to be irresponsible and impulsive. Seeking Safety offers lessons that a therapist can use in either an individual or group setting to teach twenty-five different topics—each with an associated skill that can help restore one of those ideals. In these lessons, the person with PTSD/SUD will learn how to make changes with regard to thoughts or beliefs (cognitive skills), behavior (behavioral skills), or relationships (interpersonal skills). There are also some general or introductory lessons in this program. Seeking Safety begins by helping the PTSD/SUD sufferer:

- Give up abuse of substances
- Reduce suicidal thoughts
- End dangerous relationships, such as one where there is domestic violence or the PTSD/SUD sufferer's friends abuse substances
- Gain more control over the symptoms of both PTSD and SUD

The second phase of treatment will likely include exposure therapy and cognitive restructuring, two therapeutic approaches that, while they have been successfully used to treat many PTSD sufferers, are not recommended for all PTSD sufferers. Both approaches fall under a larger category of therapeutic approaches known as cognitive behavioral therapy, or CBT. CBT helps people change how they think and behave. Again, while CBT is used to treat PTSD, not all CBT approaches are appropriate for all cases of PTSD; you must look at the nature of the trauma that resulted in PTSD as well as other coexisting problems.

By the way, while you might prefer to deal with relationship and occupational issues early on, they are typically dealt with during the third treatment phase of Seeking Safety.

Treating PTSD on Its Own

If your partner suffers only from PTSD and is primarily plagued by nightmares, flashbacks, and avoidance issues because of a fear of triggering a flashback, he may want to begin the psychotherapy process with exposure therapy. This therapeutic approach rewires the brain so it's not so easily triggered. Currently, when your loved one's brain sees a pattern similar to what was present or took place at the time of the traumatic event, it may set off a flashback. After treatment with exposure therapy, this should stop happening—or should happen much less frequently.

When using exposure therapy, the therapist slowly immerses the PTSD sufferer back into the traumatic incident. To accomplish this, the therapist may have your partner actually return to the scene of the traumatic event or attempt to do something he has been avoiding, such as visiting a crowded shopping mall. The therapist will help your partner work up to this. For example, if the goal is for your partner to walk through the mall without getting nervous, the therapist might suggest that he first go to a store elsewhere that has just a few customers. When your partner can do that and feel safe, the therapist will probably suggest that he do the same thing at a slightly more crowded store. Then he may be encouraged to go to an even more crowded place yet. After doing all these things without distress, your partner will finally head for the mall.

The therapist may also have your loved one bring forth images mentally associated with the trauma. To accomplish this, your partner may be asked to talk about the incident time and again over a matter of weeks, adding greater detail each time; to write about the incident, also in more and more detail; or to watch a video that replicates something close to what your partner he went through. When your partner is able to deal with all the memories without becoming upset or emotionally overwhelmed, exposure therapy will be complete. To reach this point could easily take a dozen sessions or more.

There are several approaches that use exposure therapy to great success.

Prolonged Exposure Therapy

Dr. Edna B. Foa, the founder and director of the Center for the Treatment and Study of Anxiety at the University of Pennsylvania and one of the leading experts on PTSD and its treatment, developed the Prolonged Exposure (PE) program. As with Seeking Safety, this program has a manual for the therapist as well as a workbook—available online at *www .amazon.com* or through Oxford University Press—for the PTSD sufferer.

Prolonged Exposure therapy is divided into three parts, and it is typically delivered in eight to fifteen sessions of ninety minutes each, offered once or twice a week. In the first session, your partner will learn about typical reactions to trauma and why chronic difficulties often follow a traumatic event. In the second part of the program, he will engage in exercises whereby he relives the trauma within his mind as explained in the previous section about exposure therapy. During the third part of this treatment program, your partner will go out into the world and do things that his PTSD-impacted brain has been leading him to believe are unsafe.

As a result of going through Prolonged Exposure therapy, your partner should notice a reduction in all three categories of PTSD symptoms.

Virtual Iraq

Virtual Iraq, an approach for treating returning soldiers with PTSD, is a modified version of Full Spectrum Warrior, a popular video game. While this program may not yet be available at all Department of Defense (DOD) or Veteran Administration (VHA) facilities, it is becoming popular with the young men and women who developed PTSD after combat duty in Iraq. It should become more widely used as both the DOD and VA train more therapists in its effective administration.

With this software, the therapist is able to create an experience similar to what your partner may have experienced in Iraq—including visuals, sounds, and even smells. The therapist will start with a simple scene, talk to your partner about what he experienced at the time of the trauma that resulted in the most troubling nightmares or flashbacks, and then keep adding these gradually into the virtual scene—until your partner is able to remain immersed in the virtual scene without experiencing much arousal. Again, it may take a dozen or more sessions for your loved one to get to the point where arousal is practically nonexistent. Still, usually by the fifth session most veterans realize they're becoming less reactive to things in their real-life environments. At this point, the therapist might ask your partner to start making changes in real life—such as driving a car on a busy street or going to the crowded mall.

Eye Movement Desensitization and Reprocessing

Eye movement desensitization and reprocessing (EMDR) also changes how the PTSD sufferer reacts to memories of trauma. The therapist has the individual talk about the trauma, while simultaneously focusing on distractions the therapist creates using primarily hand movements. However, research suggests these resulting eye movements are unnecessary to treatment success. EMDR apparently works because the PTSD sufferer talks about the traumatic event—or because this approach incorporates exposure therapy. Because some people experience immediate success with this approach, and because there are a fair number of therapists trained to conduct it, your partner may want to try this first. If it proves inadequate, then she can move on to Prolonged Exposure therapy.

Imagery Rehearsal Therapy

This approach is based on the idea that when nightmares come into being via a traumatic event, they're like bad habits that must be intentionally broken. Imagery rehearsal therapy (IRT) involves rewriting a nightmare so that it has a positive outcome. Here are some instructions to share with your partner:

1. Pick one nightmare to focus on.

2. Get into a relaxed state using deep-breathing exercises. In deep breathing, you can breathe in through either your nose or mouth—although you might be more aware of how deep those breaths are when you have an open mouth. Make sure your abdomen expands outward when taking in air. Then, let it cave inward when you blow that air out again.

3. Write down what happens in your nightmare in the order that events always unfold. Include as much detail as possible about the objects present, the smells smelled, the sounds heard, etc.

4. After writing the nightmare down in detail, create a new peaceful ending. To do this, get into a relaxed state by using deep breathing again. Then, allow the words to flow from deep within you onto the paper. Trust that this will happen—don't struggle to consciously come up with an answer. Do not stop and edit as you write. Once you've completed your writing, you can modify it if you must, ensuring that it's a pleasant ending with no violent thoughts or actions.

5. Each night after getting into bed, close your eyes and see this new story unfolding in your mind as a movie. Then get yourself ready for immediate sleep by doing some deep breathing. Your goal is to calm yourself so you can drift right off to sleep after playing out this peaceful ending in your mind.

6. After this nightmare has stopped recurring, repeat the process with any other nightmares.

Encourage your loved one to try this technique for more than just nightmares. It can also help her with intrusive thoughts that cause arousal. You may even find it beneficial for yourself. Use it to erase angry scenarios that play out in your head with regard to the presence of PTSD and its impact on your relationship.

Cognitive Restructuring

Cognitive restructuring is one of the cognitive behavioral approaches that can help the PTSD sufferer—and you as well. It's useful for all sorts of people who could benefit by changing their current thinking about themselves and their world. After a traumatic experience, an individual typically thinks about her relationship to the world differently. Common thoughts include:

- The world is a dangerous place.
- People aren't trustworthy.
- I can't handle my life anymore.
- I can't do anything about my symptoms or how I react.
- I'm at least partially to blame for what happened to me and deserve all the bad stuff that's happening to me now.
- No one could possibly understand what I've been through.
- I feel so guilty because I escaped while others died.
- I will never be the same again.
- My life is ruined.
- If I weren't so weak (or lazy or worthless), I would be over this by now.

This type of thinking can promote even more negative thoughts, keeping PTSD symptoms in place. However, these

symptoms may lessen—or go away completely—after the sufferer engages in cognitive restructuring.

Your partner's therapist will help your partner understand
the meaning she has been attaching to situations that have
resulted in fear and anxiety. The therapist's goal is to help your
partner develop a more realistic appraisal of the world and
her role in it so your loved one is better able to cope with and
recover from PTSD. The therapist will also help your partner
come up with new beliefs or statements that are more likely to
produce the desired results.

So, is this the same thing as positive thinking? No, cognitive restructuring isn't just about trading negative thoughts
for positive ones. Instead, it helps the individual recognize the
errors in logic that continue to cause distress. Once these errors are corrected, she will start to think in a more reasonable
and objective way. What she thinks will come to reflect reality
more accurately.

EXERCISE CHANGING PROBLEMATIC THOUGHTS

Here are questions a therapist might ask your partner—
or even you—about beliefs or thoughts you both have regarding PTSD. If these thoughts are proving problematic
for you, your partner, or the relationship, the therapist will
help you to change them. The therapist's questions might
also enable you to change your thinking in a way that
helps you to become more supportive of your partner—
or to back off and take better care of your own needs in
addition to those of your loved one. Go ahead and try to
apply the questions below to a thought you suspect ➤

may currently be getting in your way and making it more difficult to cope with your relationship.

- What evidence do you have for this thought?
- Could there be an alternative explanation?
- What might someone else think about this same situation?
- Are your judgments based on how you felt rather than what you did?
- Are you setting yourself up for an unrealistic and unobtainable standard?
- Are you forgetting relevant facts or focusing too much on irrelevant facts?
- Is this an example of all-or-nothing thinking?
- Are you overestimating how much control and responsibility you have (or had) in this situation or matter?
- What would be the worst thing that could happen if you chose to _____ (state the action you or another is hesitating to take that probably needs to be taken)?
- What are the probable consequences of the situation?
- Are you underestimating what you can do to deal with the problem or situation?
- Where is the logic in your thought or thinking? ■

After going through the previous exercise, you should have a better understanding of the types of things your partner may be experiencing in therapy. Also, while you may not benefit from some of the approaches used with the PTSD sufferer, such as exposure therapy, cognitive restructuring can help anyone who has thoughts that are blocking him or her from getting desired results. Indeed, sometimes all you need to do is change your thinking to change your life!

————————— CASE STUDY —————————

Joy

Are you interested in how a therapy session using cognitive restructuring may unfold? Let's use an example that is centered around something called survivor's guilt. Many a PTSD sufferer endures this after being in the midst of an accident, a disaster, or a battle where he or she survived but others died.

Joy survived a fire—followed by an explosion—at the place where she worked. However, many of the people she had worked with did not make it out alive. Joy had tried to get her coworkers to leave the building with her, but since the fire was initially small, they weren't as worried about getting out as she was.

Joy: *I should have died.*

Therapist: *What have you been thinking or telling yourself about that day? See, I suspect you're having thoughts that are feeding your feelings of guilt.*

Joy: *I should have done more.*

Therapist: *Could you be overestimating what you could have done, or what your responsibilities were in the situation?*

Joy: *My parents taught me as a child that, in case of a fire in our home, to just take responsibility for getting myself out as quickly as possible.*

Therapist: *You essentially did what you had been trained to do, didn't you?*

Joy: *Yeah, I snapped right into action while others lingered. I tried to drag a few along, but they wanted to hang back like it was no big deal. But then, suddenly there was this huge explosion. They were trapped, whereas I was already into an area of the building that didn't get so damaged.*

Therapist: *And you just kept walking.*

Joy: *Actually, I was flying down those stairs.*

Therapist: *It sounds like you did a great job of taking care of yourself in the midst of this disaster.*

Joy: *And the others did not. But I sometimes think if I'd only stayed and argued with them longer, more of them might have survived.*

Therapist: *Where's the evidence that would have happened?*

Joy: *I guess there isn't any. Actually, if I'd done that, I may have been there when the explosion came—and then I would have died without saving a soul.*

Therapist: *If you were to ask your husband if you should have died, would he agree that would have been a good thing?*

Joy: *Of course not.*

Therapist: *Why not?*

Joy: *Because he would have missed me. He also depends upon me a great deal. His life would have been a lot tougher if I'd died.*

Therapist: *Do you think that the next time you think this thought about how you should have died, you could remind yourself that you have a husband who loves you, depends upon you, and is grateful you are still here? In fact, do you think you could trade feeling guilty for feeling grateful that you're alive instead?*

Joy: *Yeah, maybe I could do that.*

In this example, did you notice the type of questions the therapist asked to create a shift in Joy's thinking? And because Joy was ready to perceive what she had done differently—and not to condemn herself, but to embrace gratitude instead—there's a good chance she'll move away from this emotionally painful place she has been living in. Hopefully, she will find life more pleasant in the future.

The Sexual Assault Survivor

If your partner has PTSD stemming from sexual assault, there are other treatment approaches you should be aware of. You should also be aware that sexual trauma can result in physical issues as well as psychological ones. If your partner is a woman, she may suffer from irritable bowel syndrome (IBS), pelvic pain of unknown origin, painful menstruation, headaches, frequent vaginal infections, and other gynecologic disorders. She may also feel less healthy or positive about her health than a woman who has never been sexually abused. The woman who has a history of childhood sexual abuse may also have more severe mental health issues than the woman who experienced a single incident of sexual assault in adulthood. Realize that this type of history can result in depression, suicidal thoughts, and perhaps even a personality disorder.

Certainly, if your partner is experiencing health issues, she needs to see a good primary care physician whom she trusts. She also needs to make this professional aware of her history. Furthermore, whenever she is referred to a specialist, she should remember that the new doctor may not be aware of this potentially important information nor inquire about this aspect of her health history. So, encourage your partner to be assertive and bring it up on her own. It may help her health care provider to understand and treat problems that may seem inexplicable otherwise, perhaps even after many expensive tests.

Multiple-Channel Exposure Therapy

Multiple-channel exposure therapy, or MCET, is used to treat panic attacks and PTSD. Since these conditions often occur together in rape victims, MCET may prove more helpful for your partner who was raped than exposure therapy. That's because someone who is experiencing panic attacks may not be able to initially handle what exposure therapy demands of the PTSD sufferer. With MCET, she'll learn techniques to reduce her panic symptoms before she begins the emotionally challenging trauma exposure work.

Once your partner can manage her panic attacks, the therapist will probably have her write about the recent sexual assault. Next, she'll be helped to change her thinking so she can better deal with the trauma. Once she has processed the sexual assault in these ways, she'll likely begin exposure therapy to learn to deal with all the sights, sounds, smells, and locations associated with the sexual assault.

MCET was developed to treat survivors of domestic violence, physical assault, and rape. Nonetheless, therapists have made an adaptation for rape victims specifically. Sometimes it is offered in group sessions instead of merely individual therapy sessions. If MCET is offered in such a setting and your partner is considering attending, she should inquire if participants are all sexual assault victims. Because your partner likely has guilt and shame issues that victims of other types of violence do not, she will probably feel more comfortable in a group of sexual assault survivors only.

Cognitive Processing Therapy

Cognitive processing therapy (CPT) combines elements of exposure therapy and cognitive restructuring. It positively impacts both PTSD and depression in female sexual assault survivors. As with MCET, it seems effective whether the sexual assault victim is exposed to this approach in a group or an individual setting. In this approach, the PTSD sufferer is asked to write about the sexual assault in detail—as well as the meaning of the assault to her. She is asked to discuss how it impacted her feelings of safety, trust, power, esteem, and intimacy, for example. After that, she'll be encouraged to read and reread the narrative until telling her story is no longer so emotionally upsetting—until the painful memories lose their hold on her.

If your partner engages in CPT, she'll also be educated about how her thinking affects her emotions. Most likely, she'll be asked to identify specific things that she has been thinking that keep her from putting the traumatic event behind her. For example, she may realize that she's been blaming herself for the assault. To move forward, she may need to come up with new thoughts that lay responsibility on the perpetrator, not herself.

Stress Inoculation Training

Ever since the sexual assault, has your partner been plagued by fear and anxiety more than anything else? If so, she may be a good candidate for stress inoculation training (SIT). SIT has three phases: education, skill building, and application.

First, your partner will learn how fear develops as a response to trauma. Next, she'll be asked to identify things that trigger fear in her. She will then learn the skills needed to control her fear reactions. Examples include deep breathing, progressive muscle relaxation, thought stopping, cognitive restructuring, and any other cognitive or behavioral skills required to reduce her fear and anxiety levels. Usually these skills are taught over ten to fourteen sessions presented in a seven- to fourteen-week period.

Now that you know the types of treatments that are available, let's talk about how you find the right therapist to conduct these therapeutic interventions.

Chapter 4

Finding the Right Therapist for Your Partner

69 Does Your Partner Feel Comfortable?

70 When the Going Gets Rough

71 Pay Attention to Style

72 Professions, Professionals, and Licensing

74 Other Professionals

75 Finding a Therapist with PTSD Expertise

78 The Family Physician

78 Making Contact

Your loved one can likely be helped if he receives the right kind of therapy—and you're committed to making sure this happens. But with the myriad therapists out there, whom should your partner select? You don't want him to waste valuable time with the wrong therapist.

If you're approaching prospective therapists, it's important to be honest about all the issues your loved one faces. If he suffers from PTSD, SUD, and depression, tell the therapist. If your partner abuses multiple forms of substances, name each and every substance used. After all, even a therapist who has the skills needed to treat PTSD may be uncomfortable tackling the other issues. It's best to know this immediately so you don't waste precious time and money on the wrong therapist. You also don't want your partner to get discouraged about therapy because he was sent away from an office or, worse yet, the therapist tried to treat him despite lacking the skills or experience necessary to tackle his issues.

Don't be afraid of having someone turn down your partner as a client. Believe and trust that you will find someone else. However, the two of you may reach the point where you're inclined to see almost any therapist because, quite simply, the process of finding a good therapist seems time-consuming and tiring—especially with everything else you have to deal with already. This is understandable, but remind yourself that the right therapist can mean the difference between success and frustration.

It may be challenging or embarrassing for the two of you to lay everything out in front of a stranger. You partner might harbor feelings of guilt associated with the trauma, especially if he is a victim of sexual assault or a war veteran. If this rings true for you and your partner, remind yourselves that experienced therapists have heard all sorts of things; their role is to offer support and guidance—not to judge.

Of course, talking about these things might prove difficult if either of you has remained in denial about what's been going on. It's emotionally painful to focus on the realities facing the two of you, but it must be done to get to a better place. Remember, while most problems tend to stick around without intervention, many grow even worse—especially for the PTSD sufferer.

If the two of you aren't up-front with the therapist, she may never fully comprehend everything that's going on. Therapists are trained to begin with the issues the client raises, and although they should ask questions to see if other issues exist, clients often minimize PTSD and SUD, probably because of guilt and shame. Because doing this won't help solve your problem, both you and your partner should be proactive and speak up.

Does Your Partner Feel Comfortable?

Your partner needs to find a therapist whom he is able to trust. Of course, he might not be comfortable with any therapist initially; this is to be expected because he is likely uncomfortable with the therapy process itself at this stage. To help your partner get beyond this, remind him that the therapist is not there to act as a best friend. This is a professional relationship. Also, the license under which the therapist practices restricts the therapist's behaviors. Licensing boards are concerned about protecting both the client and the therapist and nothing should come to pass that allows either the therapist or client to view their relationship as being anything other than professional.

Still, if your partner continues to feel uncomfortable and distrustful even after a few sessions, he may want to try a new therapist. However, the more complex the case, the fewer options there might be, and so your partner may do better to stick with someone who isn't a perfect fit rather than giving up on therapy. But if there are options, he can go ahead and try someone else. Just be aware that if every therapist makes your partner uncomfortable, it could be that he is struggling with the process of therapy itself. Indeed, he may unconsciously be using discomfort with the therapist as an excuse to give up on the therapeutic process.

When the Going Gets Rough

It may be helpful to remind your partner that therapy isn't typically easy for anyone. A person may go to a few sessions and find instant relief, but there will be other sessions where things will be demanded that will take the sufferer into painful territory. Your partner will be asked to deal with the painful memories that he has likely been struggling to squelch. As a result, he may feel that he is walking into the darkness and will be left there to struggle alone.

Your partner needs to realize that it's normal to take a step backward now and then. Also, therapy is never a straight upward pathway into the light. If your partner is truly feeling emotionally overwhelmed, though, the therapist needs to know this. Your partner should talk to the therapist openly and honestly about what's being experienced, and then pay close attention to the therapist's reaction.

Does the therapist hear your partner out? Is she willing to make changes to accommodate the needs of your partner? If so, your partner should probably continue on with this therapist—maybe at a slower pace than before. But if the therapist won't listen and charges forth with a one-size-fits-all approach to therapy, perhaps it is time for a change of therapist—but certainly not an end to therapy!

Right now, let's look at how your partner can avoid ending up with the wrong therapist.

Pay Attention to Style

A therapist may have a style that's a bad fit for one client, but a great fit for another. Some therapists adhere to what is called the medical model, where the person seeking services is seen as sick while the therapist has the responsibility, expertise, and tools to cure the problem. The client is expected to remain compliant and follow orders.

If your partner is a veteran, she may be used to following orders—and may feel quite comfortable with this approach. In fact, she may feel uncomfortable with a style that many therapists embrace today where the therapist makes the client a partner in his treatment—helping to determine and direct the treatment plan. Such therapists see their clients as having expertise in themselves and their needs. And in fact, in the long run this attitude and approach seems to be more effective.

You and your partner should also pay attention to how observant the therapist is, how comfortable she is dealing with feelings, how insightful she is, and the degree to which she can hear painful or seemingly unspeakable truths. All of these things will impact how successful the therapy sessions will be for your partner with PTSD.

You can probably appreciate the importance of all these traits when you realize that your partner will need to talk about painful things around which hurt, fear, guilt, and shame may swirl. The therapist must evoke trust. Your partner needs to feel that he will be heard no matter what horrors he may reveal. He needs to know that he won't be judged, but will be helped and treated with compassion.

The therapist should do things to help your partner feel more confident and capable. To promote these feelings, the therapist should ensure that the two of them work together to determine your partner's primary needs, and then to forge a treatment plan that offers your loved one the chance to make the improvements that she most desires—which may or may not fit with what the therapist thinks should take priority.

Of course, if your loved one's wishes aren't in alignment with what may best promote a life free of PTSD symptoms, ideally, he will see the wisdom of deferring to the therapist. If a relationship of understanding and trust exists between your partner and the therapist, your partner should be able to hear what the therapist recommends and take that advice. It should also become easier for your partner to move forward and take any necessary steps once she understands why certain actions are needed.

Professions, Professionals, and Licensing

Now that you have an idea regarding the style of the therapist that your partner may prefer, are you wondering which of the myriad professionals out there—all licensed to provide psychotherapy—may prove most effective for him? Because you're dealing with PTSD, the universe of psychotherapists you probably want to spend your time investigating is limited. That isn't to say that someone outside this universe may not have the skills you need. But your time is best spent looking in two groups where such therapists are most likely to be found.

To get started in your search, check out clinical psychologists or clinical social workers and find those with expertise in exposure therapy, cognitive restructuring, or any of the methods that your partner is likely to need. The clinical psychologist should have a PhD or a PsyD, and needs to be licensed as a psychologist. The clinical social worker may have a PhD or DSW, but is more likely to have a master's degree in social work as well as licenses that allow her to perform as a clinician.

A social worker may have a license that mandates that she practice under the supervision of another social worker or one that allows for independent practice. Typically, someone from the latter group will be more experienced because she will have had to work under the supervision of a licensed practitioner for two or three years before being allowed to take the test necessary to get her own license. However, spelling out what the resulting license will be—the letters that appear after the social worker's name—is difficult to do here since the designations for the two clinical practice levels can vary by state.

A clinical social worker must follow certain rules of practice as defined by the Association of Social Work Boards (ASWB). At its website (*www.aswb.org/members_reglinks.shtml*) you can find links to the various rules and statutes for each state. If your partner is seeing a psychologist, you can access the rules of practice for each state through the Association of State and Provincial Psychological Boards at *www.asppb.net*.

Your partner will probably contact several therapists before making an actual appointment. He should feel free to ask each therapist about his or her degrees and licenses. However, realize that the fact that someone is working in an agency with the minimal level of licensing for practicing as a clinician doesn't tell you too much. That person could have more experience with PTSD than a therapist with a private practice. In fact, often therapists working in public agencies do have more experience dealing with complex mental health issues than those out there on their own. Many therapists in private practice see clients who don't have significant problems in their lives such as PTSD and SUD. So, when you and your partner are choosing a therapist, ask questions and find out how this therapist would approach someone with PTSD, SUD, or whatever problems your loved one faces. But if you discover a therapist who seems unwilling to answer your questions, you may want to thank him and then go ahead and call the next therapist on your list.

Other Professionals

Certainly, there are other types of professionals who can provide therapy besides those I've listed. If your partner is a religious individual, she may feel inclined to seek out a pastoral counselor at your church. If she is plagued by feelings of guilt because she was in a war zone and did things against her personal religious upbringing, a pastoral counselor might prove quite beneficial. Still, pastoral counseling should be pursued in addition to—not in lieu of—the cognitive behavioral therapies such as exposure therapy and cognitive restructuring. Your loved one needs the primary therapist to be someone who has real expertise dealing with PTSD and its symptoms.

Perhaps the pastoral counselor could join this primary therapist and become part of the treatment team.

Also, after your partner has her symptoms under better control, the two of you may decide to work on the damage PTSD has wrought on your relationship by seeking out a marriage and family counselor. This person may be a licensed professional counselor instead of a clinical psychologist or clinical social worker. Or if your partner is facing career issues, she might want to see a counseling psychologist who specializes in testing people for job aptitude and can provide career guidance.

So, although there are other professionals out there who can be of benefit to your partner, while the two of you are initially confronting the realities of PTSD, stick with someone with real expertise managing this disorder. And remember, if you're looking for a therapist who can provide guidance on how to better cope with your partner, you'll probably be best served by scheduling sessions alone with your partner's therapist, as another therapist may not comprehend what you are truly facing.

Finding a Therapist with PTSD Expertise

Typically when trying to find a good therapist, you'd talk to people you know to see if they can recommend someone they liked. This may work if you're in need of someone with expertise in marital or family therapy, but the two of you need a trauma therapist who can treat PTSD and its accompanying issues. While your psychiatrist or family physician may have some ideas, you may want to use the Internet and make some phone calls to facilitate your research. Here are some places to get help with your search:

- **Anxiety Disorders Association of America**
  (*www.adaa.org/GettingHelp/FindA Therapist.asp*)
  Put in your zip code and the distance you're willing
  to travel. You'll find psychologists, social workers, and
  nurses who may have the expertise to help your partner
  with PTSD.

- **Association for Advancement of Behavioral and
  Cognitive Therapies** (*https://abct.org/members/
  Directory/Clinical_Directory.cfm*)
  Conduct a search for PTSD. You should discover close
  to five hundred names. If your loved one has other issues, check off those as well. Remember, it is best to
  locate someone who specializes in all of the problems
  your partner has. While it may take a little time to
  find someone qualified near you, it should be worth the
  trouble, as these people are the type of specialists you
  need.

- **American Psychological Association**
  (*http://locator.apa.org/results.cfm*)
  Put in your zip code and the distance you are willing
  to travel, and you'll be given a list of psychologists.

- **National Association of Social Workers**
  (*www.helppro.com/aspdocs/naswbsearch1.asp*)
  Put in your state, agree to the terms, and then indicate
  your zip code, the distance you're willing to travel, the
  type of expertise you're looking for, and other relevant
  information.

- **United States Department of Human Services Substance Abuse and Mental Health Services Administration** (*http://mentalhealth.samhsa.gov/databases*)

Put in your state, click on the mental health services locator, and search using your own town or one nearby. You should discover the phone number for a hospital or agency that can help you out.

- **National Center for Victims of Crime**
  This is a comprehensive database of thousands of community service agencies throughout the country that directly support victims of crime. Call their toll-free information and referral service at 1-800-FYI-CALL.

- **The Local Phone Book**
  Go to your local phone book and check out the blue government pages. In the "County Government Offices" section, look for a "Health Services " or "Department of Health Services" section. In that section, look for listings under "Mental Health." Call and ask these agencies for referral assistance. You can also check out "counseling," "psychologists," "social workers," "psychotherapists," "social and human services," or "mental health."

- **Human Resources or Personnel Office**
  If you or your partner works for a large company or organization, call the Human Resources or Personnel Office. Ask if the company has an employee assistance program (EAP) and, if so, get that number. You should not have to explain why you are asking for it. When you call the EAP, you can ask them if they can either provide mental health services or make referrals. Because this is a health program, they operate under laws that demand that they maintain confidentiality.

- **Health Maintenance Organization**
  If you're a member of a health maintenance organization (HMO), call to find out if they offer mental health services.

- **Local College or University**
  Consult a local university or college department of psychology, social work, or nursing for assistance with locating therapeutic resources.

The Family Physician

If your partner hasn't had a good physical examination in the past two years, he'll need an appointment with his primary care doctor. Make this appointment before you go to great lengths to find the right therapist. Why? Because medical illnesses can mask or contribute to mental health conditions.

Even if your partner does not consult directly with a psychiatrist, any specialist will probably require a physical exam or want to consult with your partner's personal physician before prescribing any medications.

Making Contact

When it is time to start contacting therapists, you or your partner should have a list of potential choices in a notebook or in a document on the computer. Your partner should be prepared to compile notes beside each therapist's name—answers to the questions she chose to ask. This information will help the two of you make comparisons later.

When your partner calls a therapist, the therapist will likely ask why she wants to be seen and why she's calling at this time. In other words, did something just happen that triggered this call for an appointment, or that kept your partner from waiting another few weeks to call? If the therapist suspects this is an emergency—or is on the way to becoming one—he will likely try to see your partner sooner rather than later. The therapist also knows that often a person will call in the midst of a crisis, push to be seen immediately, and then won't show up for the appointment because the immediate crisis has passed—even if it's only days later.

While on the phone, your partner should be prepared to briefly tell the therapist about the nature of the traumatic event(s), when the trauma occurred, the symptoms experienced, under what conditions the symptoms typically appear, and with what frequency. Again, if she has other complicating factors such as SUD, these need to be disclosed right away. Remember, most therapists do specialize, but if a therapist doesn't specialize in PTSD, don't just hang up the phone. Ask him to refer you to someone who may be appropriate.

―――――――――― CASE STUDY ――――――――――

Sam and Dr. Carson

Because it can be anxiety-producing to make that initial call to a therapist, here's how such a phone call might progress. Pay attention to the types of questions the caller, Sam, asks the therapist, Dr. Carson.

Sam: *Hello, Dr. Carson, my name is Sam. I'm trying to locate a therapist with expertise treating PTSD. Would you be able to help me?*

Dr. Carson: *I probably can, but tell me more about your case, Sam. Then together we can decide if I'd be a good fit for you.*

Sam: *I'm a freelance photographer. I got back about two months ago after covering some brutal stuff in Africa. My wife thinks I've changed after being there—and I need help.*

Dr. Carson: *What type of changes does she see and do you agree with her, Sam?*

Sam: *Well, yeah, because I've been having these night- mares almost every night during the last two months. I can't get a good night's sleep. Do you think you can help me, Dr. Carson?*

Dr. Carson: *I think so, Sam. It does sound like you might have PTSD—which I do treat.*

Sam: *That's great, but would you mind telling me about your credentials?*

Dr. Carson: *I'm a licensed psychologist. I specialize in anxi- ety disorders, including PTSD. The majority of my clients have trauma-related issues.*

Sam: *What type of therapeutic approaches do you use?*

Dr. Carson: *Have you heard of cognitive behavioral therapy, or CBT?*

Sam: *Yes, I've read about it.*

Dr. Carson: *The research shows that these techniques work well in treating PTSD. I primarily use two specific therapies under the CBT umbrella called exposure therapy and cognitive restructuring.*

Sam: *Dr. Carson, have you helped people with PTSD due to experiences similar to mine?*

Dr. Carson: *Sam, you'd be my first freelance photographer client, but I've certainly worked with soldiers who've seen horrific things and developed PTSD as a result of combat trauma.*

Sam: *I'm not sure if I just have PTSD; my wife thinks I have a drinking problem.*

Dr. Carson: *Have you been drinking more than usual to try to deal with your nightmares, Sam?*

Sam: *I guess I have. So, how would you handle that?*

Dr. Carson: *We'll see how severe your drinking problem is, Sam, but you may need to be hospitalized for the detoxification process. But after that, I can work with you on maintaining sobriety as well as dealing with the PTSD symptoms.*

Sam: *This sounds like a good match so far. Can you tell me what your fee is? I no longer have insurance, and my income has dropped because I haven't been able to work lately. Do you work on any type of a sliding scale?*

Dr. Carson: *Yes, I sometimes do, Sam. Let me ask you a few questions about your financial situation, okay?*

Sam answers the questions. Dr. Carson agrees to a specific fee that is less than he'd normally charge. At this point, Dr. Carson asks Sam if he has any more questions.

Sam: *Have there been any complaints filed against you with your licensing board?*

Dr. Carson: *No, not in the twenty years I've been practicing.*

Sam: *Twenty years? I was going to ask you how long you've been doing this.*

Dr. Carson: *I've been a therapist for twenty years, but I didn't get heavy into PTSD until ten years ago. Let's make an appointment for you. Then you can come in and decide if you feel comfortable proceeding. If you don't, I know a couple of other therapists you might find helpful.*

Sam: *Sounds good to me.*

After your partner meets with the therapist for the first time, you might ask him the following questions, to help him assess whether this therapist was a good fit.

- Did you feel comfortable discussing your problems?
- Did the therapist understand what you were talking about?
- Were your concerns taken seriously?
- Did the therapist treat you with respect?
- Will the therapist involve you in the development of a treatment plan for the PTSD and all your related issues?
- Did the therapist answer your questions to your satisfaction?
- Do you believe you could come to trust this person and work well together?

Hopefully, your partner will receive help soon from someone with real expertise in PTSD. However, there are other things in addition to the therapies we've discussed that can help your partner. Let's look at them next.

Chapter 5

More Possible Tools for Your Loved One

86 Deep Breathing

88 Help via Writing

89 Integrative Restoration

90 Being Helped by the Group

93 Brief Psychodynamic Psychotherapy

96 The Need for Sleep

Did you know it could take multiple approaches to help your partner get his PTSD symptoms under control and keep them that way? Think of PTSD as similar to a chronic illness such as diabetes. Your partner must do certain things regularly to keep the symptoms in check. But because PTSD symptoms are apt to worsen under stressful circumstances, it's important for him to have various tools in his toolbelt that can be pulled out and used as needed. This chapter provides examples of some that may prove helpful not only to your partner but to you and the relationship as well. Therefore, don't just become knowledgeable about them, but consider implementing them as a team—rebuilding the connection that you've lost as a couple because of PTSD's presence. Even if you're in a relatively new relationship, working on these techniques together may cause the two of you to grow closer.

Deep Breathing

We know that the right type of deep breathing can have a calming effect. After all, when we're nervous, we move into shallow breathing. This merely perpetuates the nervousness. By using deep breathing, however, it's possible to start feeling calmer quite quickly. You may have used this technique from time to time when you were nervous—for instance, before you had to give a speech or play a musical instrument at a recital.

Your partner can combine this technique with another called imaging whenever she is overwhelmed by bad memories or slipping into a negative emotional state such as anxiety or anger. Ask her to warn you if she feels the need to use these techniques so you can honor her need for silence.

EXERCISE DEEP BREATHING AND IMAGING

Begin by breathing in deeply through the nose. Expand your chest and abdomen as you do this. When you let the air out again, let it slide along the back of your throat and out through your mouth. Let your chest and abdomen collapse inward—so they are ready to expand for the next deep breath. Then, repeat this process several times. Do you feel that you're becoming more relaxed and peaceful?

Once you feel comfortable with deep breathing and know you could teach this technique to your partner, you'll want to add the imaging component of the exercise. To do this, come up with a peaceful and relaxing scene that you can easily place yourself in mentally. For example, you may elect to imagine yourself sitting on an ocean beach, listening to waves crashing against a strip of land. You breathe in the smell of salty air and feel at one with nature. A sense of peace fills your mind.

When you go to teach this to your partner, have her talk about a scene that she finds restful. Once she has this clearly in mind, the two of you can either lie down or sit quietly, whichever is most comfortable for the two of you. First, each begins to do the deep-breathing exercise. Once you're both comfortable or into its rhythm, begin to visualize the image or scene that you find personally relaxing.

Have your partner continue to do the deep breathing while clinging to the relaxing image for as long as she can tolerate doing so. Don't be surprised if she can only ➤

continue for a minute or two. However, encourage her to maintain the image slightly longer each time she tries this. A reasonable goal is ten minutes—though twenty minutes would be better yet. ■

Help via Writing

Studies have shown that writing about one's trauma can help reduce PTSD symptoms, lift depression, minimize emotional and physical pain, and reduce physical symptoms so that the trauma survivor experiences improved overall functioning. However, if the PTSD sufferer grew up in a dysfunctional family and is thus confronting a more complex case of PTSD, engaging in this activity may prove even more beneficial than for the average PTSD victim. So, if your loved one grew up in such an environment, encourage him to try this. While your partner could certainly delve into writing on his own, he may find it helpful to have some structure to this activity, such as that provided by the questions found in *The Twelve Steps: A Way Out: A Spiritual Process for Healing Damaged Emotions*. This is a paperback manual by Friends in Recovery that offers sound information in bite-size portions and asks many excellent questions that enhance self-awareness. By answering these honestly, your partner should begin to move away from thought patterns and behaviors that have perhaps harmed more than helped him and could currently be interfering with his effective management of the PTSD and its symptoms.

Before your loved one starts writing, encourage him to do some deep breathing to relax. This will also help him connect to that part of the self that can offer the most profound answers or best solutions. Your partner should think of this aspect of the self as being about love and supreme good. As a result, the things your loved one writes after connecting with this part of the self will likely be more powerful and helpful than answers written off the top of his head. In fact, he may be quite shocked afterward by the answers he wrote out.

By seeking to write about the impact of one's past from this deeper place, it becomes possible to use a horrific or traumatic event or period in one's life as the springboard for an exciting personal journey. In fact, one could ultimately become transformed from a chain of events that were set in motion by the arrival of the initially unwanted PTSD. As a result, one day both you and your partner may look back and realize that while the PTSD created painful circumstances that threatened your relationship, you both also experienced personal development and spiritual growth that you likely wouldn't have had except for PTSD and its negative consequences.

Integrative Restoration

Do you think of yoga as a form of exercise with strange positions or unusual poses? The Army has been using a different form of yoga with PTSD-impacted soldiers. It is called Integrative Restoration or *iRest*, and it incorporates yoga nidra, an ancient form of yogic meditation. Since it is done lying on one's back, even those with physical injuries can do it. Soldiers are finding iRest so beneficial that many have wanted their partners to participate in these classes with them. You may well discover that your loved one responds just as enthusiastically.

Think of iRest as designed to help the participant experience deep relaxation, impacting both the mind and the body. The user moves beyond such problematic feelings as anxiety, fear, anger, and depression as well as other problems, such as insomnia. And in the same way that writing can, iRest can help a person tap into a deeper level of the self, or to arrive at a new level of self-awareness or consciousness.

iRest promotes meditation, which often facilitates the sense that one is connected to a source or power larger than the ego self—or to an energy field, consciousness, or ground of all being from which we all arise and are never separated—despite the fact that the ego self feels and believes otherwise. But because of this new awareness, your partner may well be thrust forward on a journey of personal transformation or spiritual growth.

Since many PTSD sufferers have been harmed by things that have caused soul wounds, often what they gain through psychotherapy such as exposure therapy and cognitive restructuring is extremely necessary and helpful but is still not enough. A program such as iRest can help promote the type of spiritual healing that those wounded by the horrors of war especially need.

Your partner may be able to find an iRest group to attend in your area. If one is not available, or if your partner prefers to engage in iRest at home, it is possible to purchase the iRest materials at *www.irest.us*, a site owned and operated by Dr. Richard Miller, the developer of the Army's iRest program.

Being Helped by the Group

There's a good chance your partner may be helped by being part of a psychoeducational, self-help support, or therapeutic group. Both iRest and Seeking Safety are offered in group format, but there are other types of groups that may prove beneficial to your partner as well.

Many people benefit from being part of a group where participants are dealing with a similar problem or issue. Some groups, such as Seeking Safety, are psychoeducational; attendees are taught certain information and skills, and then they report back weekly on how they're doing with the implementation of those skills. However, your partner could also be helped by group therapy or a self-help group. The latter category includes twelve-step programs such as Alcoholics Anonymous (A.A.) and Al-Anon. The former are conducted by a therapist, typically in an office setting for fewer than eight people.

Perhaps you could offer to help your partner locate such a group. Since she may respond negatively to the idea of doing so, though, here are some things you should know:

- Most anyone is uncomfortable attending a group initially. Encourage your loved one to give it a few tries before deciding this isn't going to work.
- PTSD sufferers typically have more trouble going to groups than most people because of the PTSD symptom of avoidance. It's acceptable for your loved one to start with individual therapy and then add some type of a group after her anxiety level has lessened.
- Just because a group wasn't beneficial at one point doesn't mean it won't be later on. If your partner discovers such a group doesn't work at first, she should give it a rest but try again at a later date.
- A PTSD support group can help your loved one break free of avoidance behavior, rebuild self-confidence, gain trust, and develop new ways of looking at the self and relationships. It will be easier for her to learn how to

deal with emotions such as guilt, shame, anger, and
fear while in a group with fellow PTSD sufferers.

- Because fellow PTSD sufferers can offer your loved one
  the kind of empathy and support you and others can't,
  she will likely be better able to proceed with therapy,
  change thinking and behaviors, and move forward with
  her life after joining such a group.

- Being part of a group may require social skills that
  your PTSD sufferer lacks. She may need to work on
  these through individual therapy first.

- Group therapy led by a therapist is apt to be more con-
  frontational than are self-help groups, since the latter
  often have rules against people cross-talking or making
  comments. Of course, if suggestions are made in a self-
  help group, your partner should never feel obligated to
  act on any of these. Instead, she should adhere to the
  slogan used in A.A. and Al-Anon: Take what you like
  and leave the rest.

- There's a chance your partner may meet someone in the
  group who gets on her nerves. If this happens, remind
  her that she is attending the group in part to learn to
  change thoughts and behaviors. It is important to try
  not to get annoyed but, instead, to practice acceptance.

- In self-help groups, participants may be at different
  levels in dealing with the group's central issue. Some
  could just be stepping out of denial whereas others
  have essentially dealt with most issues. This is often
  noticeable in A.A. and Al-Anon, where the latter type
  of people attend meetings to serve as beacons of hope
  to newer members.

- If your partner was forced by war or other trauma to
  do things against her personal values, it may be help-

ful to her to be part of a self-help group where it's also possible to benefit others. This can sometimes facilitate self-forgiveness.

Finding a Support Group for Your Partner

Finding a support group for your partner will be more challenging than finding an A.A. group or Al-Anon group, which can be found in most local phone books. If your partner is a war veteran, ask about self-help groups at the VA. Otherwise, check out the Anxiety Disorder Association of America web page (*www.adaa.org/GettingHelp/SupportGroups.asp*) where you can look up support groups state by state as well as locate materials about starting a group, if this seems a good solution to the lack of available groups in your area.

There are also groups for PTSD sufferers on the Internet. Some are for all PTSD sufferers while others are especially for veterans. While having a group where your partner can meet in person with others is preferable—it will give her the feeling of being part of a supportive community, which would benefit her—this could still prove helpful.

Brief Psychodynamic Psychotherapy

If your partner has PTSD and SUD, and suffered abuse or other painful issues as a child, he may be helped by brief psychodynamic psychotherapy. This therapeutic approach can help him understand how his past has likely played a role in the development of the PTSD and SUD he faces now. In psychodynamic therapy, the emphasis is often on the individual's use of defense mechanisms. A psychodynamic therapist, for example, may notice that a PTSD sufferer is displaying a great deal of anger toward his partner even though she hasn't done anything to deserve it. The therapist may point out that perhaps the sufferer is expressing anger associated with childhood trauma toward his partner when it would be a more helpful behavior to express painful feelings in a straightforward and healthier way.

Both the cognitive behavioral therapist and the psychodynamic therapist want to help their clients change thoughts and behaviors that get in the way of achieving the relationships and lives they seek for themselves. While psychodynamic therapy could prove helpful to the PTSD sufferer with a painful childhood, it should not be the first line of attack. Make it your first priority to help your loved one find a therapist who can provide exposure therapy and cognitive restructuring. Later—after the PTSD symptoms are under better control—your partner may want to seek out a psychodynamic therapist.

CASE STUDY

Tom and His Father

Tom was raised in a household with an alcoholic father—a weekend binge drinker. During the week while he was sober, his father would often tell Tom he'd take him to the park that weekend to go on the swings. But when the weekend came around and Tom excitedly approached his father, a stranger would invariably look back at the small boy. Disgust would be stretched across Tom's father's mouth, and he would scream and accuse Tom of being a self-centered kid who didn't care about anyone else's needs except his own. After taking this verbal beating, the young boy would shuffle off to his room with his head hanging.

After this scenario played out a number of times, Tom learned that it hurt when his father let him down like this. As a result, Tom made an unconscious decision—that he would never trust his father again. If he had no expectations, he wouldn't be let down. He would not continually experience that level of hurt. Only Tom didn't leave it at that. He generalized this belief beyond his father. He came to trust only himself.

When Tom became an adult and married, he treated his wife, Kathy, as though she'd never honor her commitments. This was extremely upsetting for Kathy because she had always prided herself on her trustworthiness. Finally, one day after Tom had shown his distrust of her one too many times, Kathy put her foot down. In no uncertain terms, she told Tom that either they would go see a therapist together or she would move into a new apartment alone. Tom agreed to accompany Kathy when she made her way to the marriage and family therapist several people had recommended.

Kathy had never been able to make Tom understand what he was doing. But the therapist told Tom a story that spoke to him. The therapist explained how a young boy made a decision early on in his childhood to distrust not only his father, but other people as well. And while this was a mechanism that defended this young boy from suffering emotional pain in childhood, it came to work against him in adulthood. The woman he actually loved dearly was now threatening to leave him. Furthermore, if she did so, this man would suffer the very thing he had been unconsciously trying to avoid or defend against—the emotional pain of abandonment.

Tom got it. From that day forth, he asked Kathy to tell him whenever she felt he had just said something or behaved in such a way that suggested he didn't trust her. Kathy was happy to do this, and told Tom on more than one occasion specifically what he had said or done. As a result, Tom became more aware of this destructive behavioral pattern, let go of this defense mechanism, and saved his marriage to Kathy.

The Need for Sleep

Many Americans do not get the seven or more hours of sleep a night they truly need. This has undoubtedly been true for your loved one because of the PTSD. Yet, sleep may be one of the most important things your partner needs to manage her problematic PTSD symptoms. They may be less apt to rear their ugly heads if she gets enough sleep regularly. Reasons your partner may find it challenging to get to sleep include:

- Medical problems that interfere with sleep, such as chronic pain or stomach problems
- Fear of nightmares, or the inability to fall back to sleep after a nightmare
- Anxiety about falling asleep because of the difficulty in doing so generally, which in turn makes it even more difficult to sleep
- Alcohol or drug abuse, which makes it more difficult both to fall and to stay asleep
- A hypervigilant system and tendency to awaken at the slightest sound, which then leads to the need to get up

and check out the room or house to ensure that everything is safe and sound

Since your partner is likely having difficulty falling or staying asleep, here are some tips for the two of you to make this less of a problem in the future:

- Change your bedroom's environment. Create a quiet and comfortable sleeping area that can easily be darkened for sleep. Ensure that it is only used for sleeping and sex.
- Don't watch television in the bedroom. Do this in another room before heading to bed.
- Consider using a "white noise" machine to help block out potentially disturbing noises. A fan may also prove helpful. However, if these aren't sufficient, your partner may want to consider wearing a sleep mask or earplugs.
- Establish a set bedtime as well as getting up at the same time each morning, including on weekends.
- In the evening, avoid doing anything stressful or energizing. In fact, avoid exercise or workout routines that take place after 5 P.M., as these can interfere with sleep.
- Avoid eating anything four to five hours before heading to bed. In addition, avoid alcohol since it has a tendency to awaken one during the night. Since nicotine can keep a person awake as well, give up tobacco products at night, if not completely.
- Be aware that medications can be the culprit causing a bad night's sleep—especially if they create withdrawal effects during the night. Ask the psychiatrist if medications can be safely taken earlier in the day.

- Avoid foods or beverages in the evening that have caffeine, such as coffee, tea, cola, or chocolate.
- Wind down before bedtime by taking a warm shower or bath, or listening to soothing music.
- Once in bed, try the deep breathing and imagery discussed earlier in the chapter.
- If sleep won't come, get up and go do something boring. When sleep finally beckons, return to bed.

If sleep remains a problem for your partner after trying these techniques, make it a point to get outside more during the day. Spending time in sunlight helps to reset the body's sleep and wake cycles. It can also lift a depressed mood.

Of course, you yourself will likely benefit from things such as this that you keep encouraging your partner to do. This is fortunate, because you're facing your own emotional challenges that can damage both your mental and physical health. In fact, you may even be grieving the loss of your partner—and your relationship—as you once knew them.

Chapter 6
What Are You Going Through?

101 The Five Stages of Grief

Denial

Anger

Bargaining

Depression

Acceptance

Do you feel that you've suffered multiple losses since PTSD entered your relationship? Are you currently grieving these losses? While you may be concerned about your recent behaviors and emotional reactions to your partner's PTSD—perhaps you even suspect you're going crazy—your behavior is undoubtedly a normal reaction to what you face. In fact, you may be going through a five-stage grief process. And while it might be challenging and painful to work through these stages, it should become less so once you understand what's happening to you.

If you're in a relatively new relationship where your partner already had PTSD at the time the two of you met, this chapter may not be as applicable to you as others. Read through it anyway. It could still help you better understand some of the emotions or reactions that you may be experiencing now or could come to experience in the future. For example, perhaps there is a great deal you like about this person—despite the bothersome PTSD symptoms that show up from time to time. As a result, you may be angry that your partner has PTSD to begin with. In displaying anger, you're exhibiting the same reaction as a person in the second stage of the grief process. Then again, maybe you've done some bargaining with God as to what you're willing to do if the PTSD could only be stripped away. This is common behavior in those going through the third stage of the grief process.

When you have a better understanding of what you are going through, you may discover that you've actually been going back and forth between stages in the grieving process. In this case, you may want to seek the help of a therapist. Realizing that what you're experiencing is perfectly normal—though emotionally painful—will make it much easier to endure.

The Five Stages of Grief

Dr. Elisabeth Kübler-Ross developed the five stages of grief after working with people facing terminal illness. She discovered that, after being informed of one's pending death, the person typically entered a state of denial. This was followed by the anger stage. Next, the person entered a stage in which he bargained with God. When it became obvious this was not going to prove fruitful, he typically moved into the depression stage. Finally, if the person maneuvered successfully through the previous four stages and didn't become stuck at one of them, he would move into the stage of acceptance.

Since the time Dr. Kübler-Ross developed these five stages of grief, therapists have realized that the stages apply not only to the dying, but also to individuals who've experienced some type of significant loss—a category into which both you and your PTSD-suffering partner fit. Your losses may not be the same, but both of you could ultimately find yourselves going through the five stages of grief.

Before we delve into each of the five stages in more detail, you need to understand, as already alluded to, that not all people proceed through these stages in an orderly fashion. You may move through a stage, think that you have left it behind you forever, and then find yourself slipping back into it again. There's also a possibility of getting stuck at a stage. One person may refuse to budge from denial. Another might linger forever in the stage of anger. Still another may not move out of depression. But of course, the goal is to progress through the first four stages. Once you reach stage five, you want to remain there—not slip backward.

Denial

Denial is about not recognizing and accepting what's actually happening in your life—in this case, that your partner has PTSD and this is impacting him, you, and your relationship. You could be facing evidence every day that suggests your partner is not the man you knew before he experienced the traumatic event. But when you're in denial, you just won't face the facts. You may make up excuses or stories to try to explain such evidence away. Even if others try to confront you with the truth, you push them away. You don't want to hear it. You have your own story that you want to believe.

Even though your partner may be in a state of denial about his PTSD or other problems such as SUD, you'll likely accept his explanations for some of his problematic behaviors if you're in a state of denial. Of course it makes perfect sense that he must get up during the night to take a drink to fall back to sleep after yet another disturbing nightmare! You don't awaken to the fact that your partner wouldn't need to drink in the first place if those nightmares were taken care of—through therapy that he refuses to get. Or you may have noticed the changes PTSD has wrought, but you convince yourself that things will soon get better despite the fact that, again, your partner is doing nothing to eradicate or manage his PTSD symptoms. You may also ignore how his behavior is affecting the children. And so you can remain in your state of denial, you won't let the children talk about what they are going through. As a result, things in your household are apt to move on a downward trajectory.

Anger

An individual typically won't remain in a state of denial indefinitely, however. Instead, she moves into the next stage—

the anger stage. While this is normal, it is not a healthy place to remain for any amount of time. It is psychologically painful. The stress hormones released when you're constantly angry are damaging to the body. Furthermore, your anger is detrimental to your partner with PTSD since it makes for a stressful living environment in which those PTSD symptoms are likely to get worse, not better. Therefore, while your loved one may have to tackle anger that stems from the hyperarousal symptom of PTSD, you must learn how to deal with the anger that stems from your grief—the loss of your partner and your relationship as you knew them before.

A number of people get stuck in the anger stage. They cloak themselves in victimhood and refuse to update their wardrobes. But then, playing the role of victim appears to offer benefits some people like—such as not having to admit that you're scared or hurting. In our society, expressing anger seems more acceptable than confronting and dealing with the fear, hurt, or combination of these two emotions that fuel anger.

What type of angry thoughts is a person apt to experience while in this stage of the grief cycle? Let's look at a couple of examples.

─────────── CASE STUDY ───────────

Kara and Jimmy, Patricia and Peter

A woman named Kara is stuck in the anger stage. Her husband, Jimmy, served in the Army and is now struggling with PTSD. Kara may silently think:

Why us, God? This is so unfair. Our lives are ruined now, but neither Jimmy nor I did anything really wrong. There are so many rotten people out there, but you punish this once gentle and loving man and his caring family? Don't you realize Jimmy joined the Army because he wanted to serve his country? Isn't that a good thing? So why did he have to develop PTSD when his closest war buddies did not?

Patricia suffers from PTSD because—as a firefighter—she'd been involved in more traumatic events than her brain could ultimately handle. Her husband, Peter, is angry at her, and thinks to himself:

Why did you ever have to go into this line of work in the first place? Or at least you could have gotten out of it after we had our first kid. You always knew PTSD could happen because it happened to one of your favorite coworkers, didn't it? But no, despite the fact that it ruined not only his life but the lives of his wife and kids, you still had to stay on, didn't you? I begged you to give it up after you were almost killed that one time a building unexpectedly collapsed, but you wouldn't. You are so self-centered! Everything falls on my shoulders now and yet you scream at the kids and me. You expect us to silently put up with your mood swings. After all, you can't help it, you tell us. It's just a sign of your PTSD. Except you could help it, but you refuse to get help. Well, frankly, I'm sick of it!

Do you get the idea of what type of angry thoughts might consume the partner of the PTSD sufferer? Did these examples bring forth your own feelings of anger that perhaps you've been trying to squelch? If so, that isn't a bad thing. It may even help you with the next exercise.

EXERCISE WRITE ABOUT YOUR THOUGHTS AND FEELINGS

If your partner has PTSD, you likely have your own angry thoughts about what you face—and this should prove true whether this is an established or a newer relationship. You may be angry for reasons that you both do and don't understand. It'll be easier to move beyond this anger stage if you can come to terms with what drives your anger. So it's time to write about your anger in your personal journal. Do *not* write these things in the notebook where you're recording your partner's changed behaviors.

As you get started, avoid giving yourself a hard time about your feelings of anger; don't belittle yourself if you feel angry about things that seem trite or self-centered. Accept the fact that these are merely feelings—you don't have to act on them. However, you do need to get in touch with them so you can let them go and become more accepting of whatever life brings—the good and the bad. As you get ready to do this exercise, remember that hurt, fear, or both fuel anger. When you seek to understand and acknowledge your underlying feelings, your anger is apt to lessen—or disappear.

If you're ready to allow yourself to write about all the angry thoughts you're having about your partner's PTSD without censoring yourself in any way, pull out that personal journal and put pen to paper. Allow those thoughts that have been stifled to flow out onto the page.

After you've finished writing down those angry thoughts, go back and study the things you said. When you talk ➤

about being angry, think about what feeling was probably behind that anger. Was hurt, fear, or both fueling your anger? Write the underlying emotion in the margin beside each example of anger you wrote about.

Do you have that done? Good, because there's something else to do with the material you just wrote. ■

EXERCISE DEVELOPING THREE-PART ASSERTIONS

You may have written about things that don't pertain to your partner or your relationship specifically. For example, if your partner developed PTSD as the result of being in a war zone, you may have expressed anger at the president or the government for getting us into war. Nonetheless, there are undoubtedly other statements that do pertain to your partner and how his or her PTSD has impacted both you and your relationship. You'll use these in this exercise.

You're going to use a three-part assertion here to write what you have to say. State the behavior your partner engages in that upsets you; describe how that behavior makes you feel; and give a reason explaining why you have this reaction. In some cases, you'll need to make two different three-part assertions; one explaining the hurt and another the fear that feeds your anger. Other times one three-part assertion will be adequate because your anger is fed by hurt or fear—not both. ➤

Don't share these assertions with your partner. They're to help you get in touch with the feelings and thoughts underlying your anger and to help you become more self-aware. Someday it might be appropriate to make such statements to your partner, but not now.

Here are some examples of three-part assertions:

- When you have a flashback, I feel fear because it's scary to watch, and I don't know how to help you.
- When you won't have sex with me anymore, I feel hurt because it's as if you're saying I'm no longer physically attractive. And then, when I believe you don't find me attractive anymore, I feel afraid because I think you're going to go off and have an affair.
- When you won't talk to me about what you experienced that resulted in the PTSD, I feel hurt because it's as if you don't trust me to listen and be nonjudgmental.
- When you drink all the time, I feel fear because I don't know that I can live with the problems of alcoholism, but I love you and don't want to have to leave, either.

Are you in better touch with your own anger now? If so, let's look at the next stage of grief, bargaining. ■

Bargaining

While some remain stuck in the anger stage, most will generally move on to the next stage in the process, bargaining. In this stage, an individual is still unhappy about what has come to pass and wants things to be different. But now, the person turns to God—and tries to bargain for what she desires.

How is this played out? The person bargaining with God is likely to believe that she has fallen short of being the type of person God would have preferred. Or she might feel guilty about some past behaviors, believing that she has not adhered to her personal inner moral compass or lived up to commitments made to others. Thus, when she bargains with God, she may promise that she'll never engage in any wrongful behaviors again. For example, a woman who has engaged in one-night stands while on business trips may promise to never have such an affair again—providing God sees to it that her husband enters treatment for his PTSD and their loving relationship is restored. A man who realizes that he never was very helpful around the house may promise God that he'll help his wife out with all household chores in the future—if only God will cure her of her PTSD symptoms.

Have you been bargaining with God since your partner began suffering from PTSD? If so, get out your personal journal again. It is time to assess the meaning behind the things you've chosen to bargain about.

EXERCISE LEARNING THE LESSONS BEHIND YOUR BARGAINS WITH GOD

By studying the bargains you've been trying to make with God, you can become more self-aware. This can be looked at as the positive side of something that you may currently be seeing as entirely negative. Take the following steps:

1. Lay your journal or piece of paper on the horizontal and, down the left-hand side, list the different bargains with God that you've been trying to make lately.

2. Go down the list. Analyze each bargain one by one. Does that bargain suggest that you've been falling short someplace, somehow? Write down yes or no beside each bargain.

3. Return to the bargaining items for which you said yes. Ask yourself if you've fallen short of your own standards, values, or personal goals, or if you've fallen short of those someone else may have held for you. Write down the word "personal" or "another," depending on which category it falls into.

4. Study the bargains you've made because you realize you've failed to live up to others' expectations. Do you want to make any of these personal, or do you want to let them go? Mark each one with either "make personal" or "let go."

5. Beside any bargaining item that you want to continue to adhere to or make personal, write down one thing that you could start doing immediately that could help you better meet that standard, value, or ➤

goal. This is not to say you will meet it, but merely that you'll be taking one step—even a baby step—to move in this direction.

6. Select only one of these items to implement for the next thirty days—and do just that.

Do you feel better about yourself now that you plan to take some type of action? Also, did you learn anything about yourself that you found surprising? When you're in a relationship with someone with PTSD, things can feel very much out of control. It can be helpful to keep taking actions that allow you keep your perspective and ensure that you don't make everything out to be your partner's fault. This way, you remain in touch with the type of person and partner you want to be throughout all of this. ■

Depression

When you're depressed, the brain ceases to function properly. It feeds you bad ideas that aren't true, such as the idea that the emotional pain you're currently experiencing will last forever. It won't, but when you're depressed, it can seem as though the future is destined to unfold forever as it's currently doing. It's important to remember that these are only thoughts. They don't represent reality. Your state of depression may lead you to predict a dismal future, but none of us can predict the future accurately. We typically anticipate a certain future based upon what has happened in the past, but you can always stop and make new choices that will lead to new results.

The truth is, you can stand things the way they are. Certainly you may not like—or prefer—your current circumstances, but you can stand them. And if you think things should be different, don't just moan that they aren't. Instead, make a new choice. Decide today to start creating something different—something better. Decide upon even one baby step you can take in this direction. After all, when you're depressed, you don't have the kind of energy and focus to make lots of simultaneous changes, but you'll gain confidence by taking even one small step—and then another—in the direction you want to go. Soon, you'll see that you have the power to create your own happiness. You don't have to bemoan the fact that your partner and your relationship can't rescue you by providing all the happiness you want. You can become the creator of the happiness instead.

You may not be able to recreate the type of relationship the two of you had in the past—as much as you may desire that. If you're in a newer relationship with someone with long-standing PTSD, he may not be capable of doing or being the things you anticipated when you first met. However, the two of you may be able to forge a different type of relationship that brings its own unique rewards. Furthermore, you may grow personally and spiritually from this experience, which could be a positive that comes from this negative.

Acceptance

Acceptance is going along with whatever has shown up in your life; you neither deny it nor fight it. If you accept the fact that PTSD has shown up in your relationship, you don't sit around pretending everything is the same, but you don't sit around feeling sorry for yourself either. When you remain in a state of denial, things tend to move forward on their own course. By accepting the fact that your partner suffers from this mental disorder, you are in a position to deal with all the undesired issues.

However, just because you've accepted your partner's PTSD doesn't mean that you love what's happening. Instead, you simply realize that the PTSD is there and must be dealt with, and you decide to do the best job possible of doing that. Can you see that acceptance is not about giving up control or doing nothing? Instead, it propels you toward being proactive. Once you face up to any painful circumstances—and then go forth and do the things that will alleviate as much of that suffering as possible—you'll grow as a person. And as you do so, you'll come to have even greater acceptance for more of what life delivers—either good or bad.

The good news is that once you get into a place of acceptance, life is inclined to deliver more things that bring joy instead of what you suffered while lingering in denial. Remember, while denial may seem to work initially, it usually leads to more severe consequences and emotional pain on down the road. It's as if some power higher than the self—call it the Universe, the Ground of all Being, Consciousness, God, whatever you prefer—demands that we learn certain lessons from life experiences. If we refuse to do so, the lessons will typically become more painful yet, as if to ensure that we finally do pay attention.

You can indicate your acceptance of your partner's PTSD by starting to educate yourself about the disorder and its treatment—as you're doing by reading this book. With this knowledge in hand, you will be able to help your partner seek out the best treatment he can get. Then you could lend support while he pursues the actions demanded by his treatment plan. At the same time, you also want to take all the actions you can to help ensure your own well-being. This will provide you with the fortitude and right mental attitude to do those things that will continue to help your partner and your relationship.

Now let's clarify something acceptance is not. Acceptance doesn't mean that you must remain by your beloved's side and watch his inevitable downward spiral if he refuses to take any responsibility for PTSD, refuses to get treatment, and continues in destructive behaviors. Rather, you may accept that something different is demanded of you now. You must come to accept that ultimately, all you can control is your own self.

Your partner is responsible for himself. All you can do is offer guidance and lend support. Ultimately, if your partner is to beat PTSD, he must take certain actions on his own. The helping hand you offer is extremely important, but your partner has a personal healing path to walk. By the way, you also have your own.

Chapter 7

Take Care
of Yourself First

116 Step Off the Victim-Rescuer-
Persecutor Triangle

118 Start Focusing on Yourself

119 Finding Support

121 Asking for Help

123 Your Need for Sleep

123 Stress-Busting Exercise

125 Avoid a Bad Diet

127 Physical and Mental Health

128 Change Your Expectations

131 An Attitude of Gratitude

132 Are You Your Partner's Keeper?

You undoubtedly desire a loving relationship that's about partnership, but that's not possible right now—and won't be until your loved one's PTSD symptoms are under better control. Meanwhile, you may feel like your partner's caregiver as well as the one who must keep the home fires burning. This responsibility can become exhausting—especially if you continue to set aside your own needs for those of your loved one.

While self-sacrifice may seem like a noble thing to do, it's not emotionally healthy for you and can even have physical repercussions. This isn't to say you should stop being your partner's caregiver. She undoubtedly needs your support and help and probably can't do it alone because the PTSD symptoms won't let her. However, you must also make a concerted effort to take care of yourself while you take care of your loved one. After all, if you develop physical or mental health issues, where would either of you—or your children—be? This chapter will essentially remind you of things you probably already realize you should be doing. Consider this a gentle nudge.

Step Off the Victim-Rescuer-Persecutor Triangle

If you aren't familiar with the victim-rescuer-persecutor triangle, it plays out like this:

1. You started out seeing your partner as a helpless victim of PTSD and wanted to save her from experiencing all the negative things PTSD can bring. You've done everything you can to support and help your partner; you've made so many sacrifices and been so understanding. Only

now you're beginning to hope for a show of gratitude or thanks—whether you're consciously aware of this or not.

2. Instead, you increasingly suffer the onslaught of your partner's irritation—if not her outright rage and abuse. Suddenly, rather than feeling like your loved one's rescuer, you begin to feel like the victim of your partner's persecution.

3. Your own irritation begins to grow. How dare your partner treat you this way after all you've sacrificed and done for her! You may also stop feeling supportive and no longer want to do all you can to make the home environment calm and conducive to her needs as a PTSD sufferer. Now, you likely no longer absorb your partner's slings and arrows—at least not without shooting some of your own back.

4. Your partner now turns around and proclaims herself the victim of your abuse. While it was your intent to play the role of rescuer, your partner now professes you as her persecutor.

5. Accused of being a persecutor when you feel that you've been the noble martyr, you come to perceive yourself as victimized. You label your partner your persecutor while she sees you in the same light.

6. Life on the victim-rescuer-persecutor triangle marches on its downward path toward individual and relationship destruction.

You need to step out of this triangle. You may need to give your partner the space to either succeed or fail on her own—especially if all your offers of help seem to be creating animosity. After your loved one has struggled for awhile without your help, perhaps you can gently let it be known that you're still there to assist in any way you can—because you believe that if the PTSD is successfully tackled and managed, you might enjoy a true partnership once again. Essentially, you're letting your partner tell you what is needed rather than just stepping forth to take charge of her destiny.

Start Focusing on Yourself

It's time for you to step back and focus more on yourself. Take note of what has happened to your own life since PTSD walked into your relationship. Have you become as socially isolated as your partner? There's a good chance you have. Perhaps, because you were so busy attending to your loved one's needs, you professed to be too exhausted to meet with family and friends. You may also have stayed home because you didn't feel right leaving your partner alone while he avoided people, places, and events because of his PTSD.

It may also have been more comfortable to settle in alone at home because you were suddenly facing all these emotions you didn't know how to deal with. There may have been bad feelings about your partner. You may have felt frustration and anger about what had become of your relationship. And frankly, there may also have been cheek-burning shame from feeling like a failure because of how things had deteriorated between the two of you. You didn't want to face others because you didn't know what you'd say to them. Did you dare tell the truth when you felt helpless and hopeless, and wondered how much longer you could manage when each day made you feel more overwhelmed than the last? Did you dare talk about how one day you felt like the unappreciated saint and the next day you were the one shouting at your partner like someone gone mad?

Perhaps you don't believe your family and friends can give you the type of support you need because you don't see how they could possibly understand. You may also not know how to educate them as to how they can give you the kind of support that would serve you best. That's okay. Seek out support right now from unlikely faces in unlikely places instead.

Finding Support

If your partner is drinking to self-medicate PTSD symptoms, you may want to look in your phone book and find an Al-Anon meeting to attend. There you'll find many people who understand the pain of seeing one's life and dreams shattered by a loved one's growing relationship with this chemical substance.

It may seem strange at first to attend Al-Anon and make friends with people from such a group. You may also be worried that other friends and family might discover that your life and relationship aren't perfect if they meet the people you've come to know through Al-Anon. If you're having such thoughts, remind yourself that most people have some type of family secret they're hiding. However, you may also discover that, when you admit the challenges you and your partner are facing because of the PTSD, others may actually breathe a sigh of relief. This will give them permission to lower their masks of happiness and, perhaps, to share some heavy burdens that they've been struggling to carry alone. In fact, they may have felt compelled to keep up a good front because your life seemed so perfect.

However, let's suppose that isn't what happens. What if your worst fear is realized, and one or more of your current friends disappears after you share the truth of your life. Try not to be upset. Instead, realize that your old friend is obviously not at a place in her personal journey where she is capable of being there in the way you need her to be right now. This doesn't make either of you bad people. Trust that other people will soon come into your life who'll be appropriate for the stage you're entering now.

It can be painful to lose certain friends, since your past also seems to disappear with them. But this might not be such a bad thing after all. Remember, the past is past, but life is lived in the present. Also realize that often you won't understand the role a certain person played in your life until you look back at that relationship—and sometimes not until a significant passage of time. Then you can be grateful that person was in your life to help you learn certain things and to further your personal growth. It was okay that the two of you parted, and that you each moved down separate paths.

So again, let friends and family walk away in peace. Let go of any anger that lingers and, instead, take hold of gratitude. Get out there and make friends at places where there are people who understand what you're going through. Talk to some of the old-timers who are there to offer hope and guide new people like you; see if they can tell you how you might ask your supportive family members and friends for the type of help you really need. Remember, even if your friends and family are saying and doing annoying things, it's likely not out of ill will. They undoubtedly have good hearts, but need to be educated as to what your needs and wants are, and how they can best help you meet them. Remind yourself that just as this is new to you, it's new for them as well.

Asking for Help

You not only have to learn how to ask for help, but you also need to learn how to be a gracious receiver. Just as it's likely been hard for your partner to accept your help with gratitude, you must learn how to accept help without having your feelings of worth diminished. After all, if you make yourself feel rotten because you're not capable of doing it all, you're more likely to bite the hands of those trying to help you—which will give them a good reason to walk away.

If you're struggling to ask for help, remind yourself that many people not only believe it is more blessed to give than to receive, but have reaped the rewards that come from having a generous and giving heart. Nevertheless, they may fear stepping in and offering their services because they aren't certain they'll be welcome—or they don't want to come across as viewing you as incapable of managing on your own. So, when you have a specific task that you'd love someone else to do, call and ask if that person can do it for you. Don't expect others to keep calling and asking what they can do—or to mind-read what you need done, either.

You might hesitate to ask for help because you don't know how you'll ever reciprocate. Perhaps you won't ever be able to do for these people what they did for you. But as a result of benefiting from the help of others, there's a great likelihood that in the future, you'll want to step forth and assist people in need. You may also be providing people with an opportunity to feel good about themselves. However, if a person indicates she can't help, accept that response graciously since you don't know what challenges she may be facing—such as demanding work or personal obligations. But do inquire if it would be okay to approach her again in the future before marking her off your list of people who can provide assistance.

To help others best help you, formulate a list of things they can do. One item might be as simple as having several friends send a weekly e-mail to check in and see how you're doing. You could also ask someone to go walking with you because you really need the exercise, but you can't seem to remain motivated to do this on your own. If you're a woman, you may want to get out for girl talk at least once a month. You may want to have a standing date with friends because if you don't have things planned out on a calendar, you know they may not happen. Perhaps you want to go to a support group for yourself, but don't have the energy to find one and get yourself there that crucial first time. Could one of your friends look into this for you or accompany you the first few times, to get you into the habit of going?

Sometimes we need people to help rescue us from unexpected major catastrophes. Sometimes it's just a matter of scheduling activities with others that they'd enjoy doing with or for us anyway, but without planning ahead, they just aren't going to happen. So, let others know that you can't live as spontaneously as you did before—and start asking them to commit to dates and times.

Make building your support network a priority. And don't be afraid to let people outside your family and friends help you accomplish this. Talk honestly about what you face to neighbors, coworkers, members of your church, and members of your support group, and seek out local agencies that could lend a helping hand. Don't overwhelm or bore anyone with your story, but plant some seeds and see who steps forth. If people offer to help, accept their generosity. Be that gracious receiver.

Your Need for Sleep

If you're already struggling with the stress of your changed life, lack of sleep will only make matters worse. While I've touched on this topic already—and given techniques that will work for your partner as well as you—it's important to mention it again. Remember, you can't think as clearly when you don't get enough sleep. You may become more accident-prone, or even develop illnesses such as diabetes. You know you need sleep. The question is: Why aren't you getting it? Is it because your partner is restless because he can't fall asleep? Is he getting up throughout the night to drink or take drugs? Are you fearful of your partner's nightmares because you've awakened to find him covering you with his body and calling for a medic? Or worse, have you heard stories such as a partner of a PTSD sufferer awakening to find his hands around her neck, with him seeing her as the enemy in his nightmare?

You have reason to be concerned—if not be outright fearful. While it may not be a solution you like, you may want to consider separate bedrooms. This doesn't have to last forever, but it might help you get a good night's sleep while your partner is being treated for PTSD and until those symptoms are under better control.

Stress-Busting Exercise

Were you previously exercising because it's something you're supposed to do to promote good health, a high quality of life, and longevity? Have you let this slip out of your life as you've become more and more burdened by your caregiver role? If so, make exercise a priority again. This should be easy since it probably won't require traveling or any special equipment other than some good walking shoes. It may even be something you can do with your partner because he's going to need regular exercise as well—and it will give you two some quiet time to talk.

Then again, your partner may refuse to work out with you out of fear of being forced to talk. If this is the case, you may want to establish ground rules. Make a commitment to only comment on things you notice while you're walking—or promise you won't delve into personal matters—to remove this cause of anxiety. Also, if you break the rule, allow your partner to call you on it. Then, immediately go back to honoring this agreement. Frankly, by commenting only on what you're experiencing right then, you'll be living in the moment. Since this is truly the only place where life can be experienced or lived, this is a positive thing.

Before you get started on your walk, take some deep breaths and relax. Make a mental commitment to be open to the beauty or simple pleasures that come from being outdoors. Pay attention to them as well as how alive you and your body feel while absorbing the gifts of nature about you. If your partner refuses to go with you, try to find a friend who would enjoy starting on a walking routine. Just remember, you may need to establish ground rules for walking with your friend as well; otherwise, you might want to moan and groan about the status of your life. And, while you may have a real need to get negative feelings off your chest, this may not meet your friend's needs or desires. Maybe agree that you'll have a chance to vent your feelings for the first five or ten minutes of the walk, but after that, you must switch to talking about what's happening in the moment only.

There are, of course, other forms of exercise from which you can benefit. Yoga and Pilates may be very helpful, especially if you've essentially turned your body into a suit of armor to protect yourself from your partner's verbal abuse. Both of these provide stretching, and they also promote attunement to your body—both positive things for you to seek right now. Remember, you can also lift your spirits by simply putting on some upbeat music and starting to dance around. In fact, you could go from being in a funk to feeling energetic and joyous in a matter of minutes. To ensure this can happen for you, have a couple of CDs or DVDs set aside that you enjoy moving to. This will help achieve this desired effect quickly.

Do you need more information about exercise? Would you be helped by feeling as though you're part of a program? I tend to favor the programs by the National Center of the American Heart Association (*www.americanheart.org*), but other good ones abound. If you're a woman, you may want to check out their Choose to Move program at *www.choosetomove.org*.

Avoid a Bad Diet

Some people have made junk food and sweets a lifestyle. But even if you've eaten reasonably healthy most of your life, you may be finding yourself slipping into bad eating habits now. Don't be surprised if this is the case. Your PTSD-suffering partner may be inclined to self-medicate with drugs and alcohol, but you may be doing the same thing with food. It's easy to turn to unhealthy food when you're stressed out, since stuffing your face with sweets or downing soft drink after soft drink may help you feel better in the moment. The bad news is that the initial boost from the sugar will wear off quickly, leaving you more lethargic or depressed than you were previously.

Not only will you feel worse psychologically because of the impact of the sugar on your system, but you'll likely become even more down in the dumps because of the lack of will-power you just displayed. Of course, if you gain weight from all your comfort food, it may be all the harder to love yourself. Certainly, you shouldn't feel badly about yourself if you put on some weight—or already carry some extra poundage. But why not implement ways of eating that give you more energy and the ability to handle the stress that PTSD has brought into your life—and that may cause you to lose weight, too? Here are some ways to accomplish this:

- Keep only healthy foods in your cupboards and refrigerator. Sure, you may still make trips to the cupboard hoping to find something sweet to eat, but it won't be there. You'll be forced to eat a piece of fruit, vegetable sticks, yogurt, cheese, granola, or something else that's healthy for you instead. By the way, once you've been doing this for a while, sweets won't even taste that great anymore.

- Avoid the temptation to eat out. Fix something healthy instead. It's not as time-consuming as you may think. You can actually fix simple and healthy meals in less time than it takes to get into the car and drive to that restaurant. Remember, a healthy balanced meal can be as simple as several ounces of fish or meat alongside a couple of different vegetables.

- If you still aren't sure what foods to fix so your meals are healthy, you only need to get yourself two cookbooks. Look into the one from the American Heart Association (*www.americanheart.org*), or use recipes from the American Diabetes Association (*www.diabetes.org*).

If you use these recipes before you have any health problems, you'll increase the odds that you never will!

- Grocery shop only once a week. Plan healthy meals for the week before you go shopping, and then stick to the shopping list once you're in the store.

- If you need help figuring out how to prepare healthy meals or how to prepare them while keeping costs down, check out your state's Cooperative Extension website. Do a Google search for your state's specific site by putting in that state followed by the words "Cooperative Extension." Or you can go to *www.csrees.usda .gov*. There you'll find a map where you can connect to your state's information. Then look into the Expanded Food and Nutrition Education Program, sometimes referred to as EFNEP. If your family qualifies, you could learn how to prepare economical and healthy meals—perhaps in the privacy of your home or in a small group setting.

Physical and Mental Health

By taking care of your body, you're also improving the way your mind functions. Remember, there's a connection between the two. If you get run down physically, you'll feel even more overwhelmed by PTSD's presence in your life and relationship. Furthermore, if you allow your mind to race day after day with negative thoughts that feed even more negative thoughts, you're not only going to feel mentally weak and unable, but may also become physically ill.

If you find yourself struggling, seek out help. If you go to see a physician for physical problems, be honest about what has been going on in your life. Let your doctor know just how stressful you've been finding things. He may not find a cause for your problems otherwise. But if he realizes how the mind and body are impacting each other, you may be prescribed a medication to help with the anxiety or depression. However, if you implement the strategies outlined in this book, you may start feeling better without medication, which would certainly be preferable.

Change Your Expectations

Keeping yourself mentally well is incredibly important in daily life, but especially if you're dealing with the stress of having a partner with PTSD. Often, we set ourselves up for stress and emotional pain by holding on to unreasonable expectations. You could be creating undue stress for both you and your partner by expecting your relationship to be what it was prior to the arrival of PTSD into your lives. However, if you continue to educate yourself about PTSD and its treatment, as well as try to support your partner at the level she is functioning at in the present, you're more apt to strengthen your relationship.

———————— CASE STUDY ————————

Teri and Tim

As part of his ongoing treatment for PTSD symptoms, Teri's husband, Tim, is participating in something known as skills training. Part of this training involves homework assignments — behavioral tasks Tim must do between therapy sessions. While these assignments are designed to create significant change for Tim, he is hesitant to do these things. Tim's therapist wants Tim to experience success from the start, so she wants to start Tim off with assignments that are relatively easy.

One of the things the therapist decides to work on is Tim's symptom of emotional numbing. To do this, she suggests that Tim learn some ways to better express his love for Teri. The therapist realizes that it may be difficult for Tim to go up to Teri and tell her that he loves her. While Teri has told the therapist that she doesn't know why Tim can't do that, the therapist knows that asking Tim to do this right away may be setting him up for failure. Therefore, the therapist suggests that Tim purchase a card in which he can compose his own message. Inside, he could write "I love you," or even "Thanks for always being there for me." He should then leave it on Teri's pillow.

Teri comes back to therapy the next week and reports that even though Tim did this, she was still dissatisfied. She said that because it was contrived—an assignment—it meant nothing to her. The therapist quickly points out what it had taken for Tim to fulfill that assignment. Teri's eyes are suddenly opened. She is able to change her expectations and realizes that she could even appreciate the baby steps Tim was making.

A few weeks later, Teri reports that while their relationship is still nothing like it had been before PTSD entered the picture, she now feels much better about how things are between the two of them. The therapist helps Teri see how that is because the two of them have both changed. Tim is changing his behavior while Teri is changing her thoughts—her expectations. All they need to do is keep taking steps toward changing these two things in a positive direction, and they will find their relationship growing healthier—not the way it was before, but healthier.

Many of us have been programmed to only acknowledge and value those things that make grand statements. In other words, a gift may not be valued because it wasn't expensive enough or unique enough. However, the fact that a gift was given shows thought. You would do best to try to appreciate any actions taken on the part of your PTSD-suffering partner as well. Even if the action seems contrived because it is part of the treatment regime, strive to appreciate it. Sure, you would have preferred that your loved one did something on his own volition, but please realize how this shows that your partner is attempting to make changes.

You might want to say, *I hear you. But really, is expecting my partner to tell me she loves me to my face too much to ask?* Initially, it may be. Give your loved one the gift of time to get better at expressing her love for you. And again, be grateful and happy for any such gestures you receive. If you can provide this type of positive reinforcement, the day may well come when you will have your partner looking into your eyes and expressing deep love. She may also whisper thanks for the days when you stood by, allowing her to continue to take emotionally without giving back.

It's also important for you to realize that—as sad as it might be to face and admit—your partner may never return to being the person she was before. You need to learn to appreciate her for the person she is today. After all, even if things ultimately get better, they may take a nosedive first.

Think of it like surgery. Many times surgery helps to correct a problem, but you may initially feel worse after the procedure than you did before having it. But after you've gone through rehabilitation and had time to heal, you'll likely feel better than you did before. Rather than automatically clinging to the past and demanding that things be as they were previously, spend time developing an attitude of gratitude.

An Attitude of Gratitude

Try to focus on and celebrate the good that continues to happen in your life. Focus on the good so you don't become weighed down by worry and stress. It can seem difficult at first, but you can make it a habit. Remember, even if you have to look for it, there is usually a good side or something positive that arrives out of every seemingly negative situation.

There are positive things that can come from this experience for you, too. While it's challenging, you may be discovering a side of yourself you didn't know you had. Aren't there things that you've seen in yourself since you were forced into the caregiver role that you've liked? Have you been pleased with the fortitude or patience you've displayed? And haven't you been forced to actively choose to love or act lovingly whereas perhaps this came easily in the good times? You may not have seen it this way, but in doing this, you've demonstrated a more evolved or mature form of love than romantic love. Whether your partner was or is able to receive it, you've demonstrated true love.

Please realize that almost anyone can handle the good times. It's the tough times that set the stage for personal development and spiritual growth. It's the tough times that give you the opportunity to make the grandest statements about who you are or who you desire to become. Take pride and pleasure in this strong person that you've been growing into as you've been forced to take on more of a caregiver role for your partner.

Are You Your Partner's Keeper?

To be truthful, your partner's PTSD will likely be chronic. This doesn't mean that—with treatment—the PTSD symptoms won't show improvement. However, remind yourself that PTSD presents a challenge similar to diabetes. With the proper treatment, it's possible to get both under control. But if the sufferer doesn't take the required medications, eat the correct foods, exercise regularly, and get adequate sleep, he is apt to experience problems. The thing is, you may be unable to keep your partner walking steadfastly down the right path to ensure this doesn't happen. But you can't be your loved one's caregiver forever, either.

You can help your partner to initially get the help he needs. You can be supportive so it becomes less challenging for your partner to do those things he needs to do to keep his PTSD symptoms in check. Still, there are things your partner simply has to do regularly that no one else can do for him—or make him do if he elects not to do them.

You might feel guilty as you take on more responsibility for your own life and less for that of your partner. To help alleviate this guilt, remind yourself that you can help your loved one by being a good role model for healthy and balanced living. Also, as you step forward and do things to enhance your own well-being, your partner may be encouraged to do the same, which would certainly be a very good thing.

Chapter 8
Change Your Thinking

134 Irrational Belief #1

135 Irrational Belief #2

136 Irrational Belief #3

138 Irrational Belief #4

139 Irrational Belief #5

140 Irrational Belief #6

142 Irrational Belief #7

143 Irrational Belief #8

145 Irrational Belief #9

146 Irrational Belief # 10

147 Irrational Belief # 11

148 Irrational Belief # 12

Some partners of PTSD sufferers have come to feel better about
their relationships not because their partners improved signif-
icantly, but because of the actions that they themselves took.
There's a saying that it isn't what happens to you that's important, but rather the meaning you attach to what happens
to you. In other words, what do you tell yourself about what's
happening? What is your self-talk?

Psychiatrist Dr. Albert Ellis came to realize that many people
essentially undermine their chances for happiness by adhering
to beliefs that he came to label as irrational. He identified a doz-
en of these that caused people to engage in self-talk that resulted in their experiencing some type of strong negative emotion.
Whether it was anger or sadness, for example, adherence to one
or more irrational beliefs kept these people from experiencing
or enjoying the type of lives they undoubtedly wanted.

You face challenges being with a partner with PTSD. The
thing is, if you are clinging to one or more of these irrational beliefs, you may be struggling more with this relationship
than you need to be. If you can let go of any irrational beliefs
you may have and replace then with more rational ones instead, you could completely change how you perceive your relationship. And as a result, you may come to feel better about
it without your partner doing anything at all.

Let's look at the irrational beliefs that Dr. Ellis identified.

Irrational Belief #1: I Have Certain Needs That Must Be Met

While everyone has a few basic needs to ensure survival, most
"needs" could be classified as wants. They're things we'd prefer to have, but it isn't life-threatening to be deprived of them.

Nonetheless, we turn them into matters of life and death. By doing so, we become miserable when we can't attain or sustain what was desired. If circumstances change and demand we give up something we believe we need, we're apt to experience great distress. Whatever gifts the present offers are totally ignored.

Has this irrational belief infiltrated your life because of your partner's PTSD? There may be things you've perceived as needs that are no longer being met—such as having sex so many times a week. If you want to support your partner and sustain the relationship, try to start thinking of these things as preferences or wants instead of absolute needs. As you do this, you might discover a more flexible or accepting side of yourself that has remained a stranger.

Irrational Belief #2: I Can't Stand Certain Events or Things

When you cling to this belief, you make it difficult to accomplish what you must. You may get worked up or emotional about things you can't control—such as the fact your partner has PTSD. Your negative response won't correct the situation, but it will make it more difficult to tolerate what's going on in the present. You'll also negate the chance of finding any pleasure in the moment.

You might currently be thinking that there's no way to find pleasure while living with a partner with PTSD. But that's not the case. There are things you can discover and people you can meet that will enrich your life in unsuspected ways as you try to deal with the PTSD so your partner is helped, you remain healthy, and your relationship remains as strong as possible.

You may meet wonderful people in support groups or through a twelve-step program such as Al-Anon. Indeed, people who have had to struggle with emotionally difficult experiences are likely to be more empathic than the norm; they understand that life can hand us more than we can handle alone.

Because of the challenges arising from the presence of PTSD in your relationship, you may come to grow personally and spiritually in ways you wouldn't have—not without such adversity. You may become more resourceful and creative as you develop solutions to things you now face as an individual, a couple, or a family. You may also come to see yourself as more caring than you were before. When you're confronted with something you profess you can't stand to do, but know in your heart must be done, listen to your heart. Then, argue back with that voice in your head and tell it that you *can* stand it.

To help you thrive in these trying times, collect quotations and inspirational stories that you can pull out and read whenever you're feeling down. Take some of your favorites, type them up, and frame this sheet of paper. Place it on the bathroom counter or in your bedroom where you'll see it regularly. Read these quotations before you start your day.

Irrational Belief #3: My Worth Is Determined by My Successes and Failures as Well as by the Traits I Exhibit

This irrational belief results from not believing in your innate self-worth. If you hold to this belief, you probably cannot accept your human frailties. Also, you may believe that you must always be accomplishing something to have any worth at all. As a result, you have likely achieved goal after goal, but you've found little enjoyment in the process.

If this sounds like you, it's important that you step away from the idea that unless you're a successful "human doing," you can't be a successful human being. While you may not believe it today, even if you're not a successful "human doing," you are worthy of love and respect. But then, so are others who aren't achieving constantly—such as your partner with PTSD.

If you hold to this belief, you may have trouble feeling worthy of love. And when you don't feel worthy of love, you can't really give love to others. So don't be surprised that if you cling to this belief, you might be having trouble loving your PTSD-impacted partner because he's not living up to your standards for success. Of course, before your loved one developed PTSD, everything may have been just fine. You likely felt good about yourself because you had the type of relationship you'd always wanted. You likely saw yourself as a caring and loving partner, too. In your mind, you were living on the success side of the equation. But if you've been giving yourself bad marks since PTSD has brought changes into your life and relationship that you have been unable to control or fix, perhaps it is time to give up this belief. You may be helped immensely by participating in a twelve-step program. If you go and actually work the steps, you'll likely experience the acceptance of others without doing anything that wins awards.

Start today to tell yourself you have worth merely because you walk this earth. Accept yourself as you are right now. This doesn't mean that you remain stuck or never try to change. Rather, it means embracing yourself as a wonderful person about to embark on a new journey—a journey that is currently being shaped to a significant degree by your partner's PTSD.

Irrational Belief #4: I Must Always Have the Approval of My Parents and Other Authority Figures

Is there a part of you that is still concerned with gaining Mom's and Dad's approval? This part doesn't realize that the past is past, and it still fears abandonment. Of course, abandonment is a legitimate fear for the small child since it can be paramount to death. But as an adult, you can be abandoned and still survive.

Perhaps instead of being the type of partner you want to be for your loved one, you're worried about being the type of partner you think your parents would want you to be under the current circumstances. You may feel badly about yourself if you realize that you can no longer live up to their expectations. Giving up this belief, though, may alleviate a significant amount of stress. You may eliminate lingering feelings of diminished self-worth as well. Perhaps you can't advocate for the care or benefits your partner needs because you fear what the authority figures within the hospital may think. If you give up this belief, your effectiveness as your partner's advocate will undoubtedly improve.

If you could forget about what others may think and, instead, follow the urging of your heart, you could heal your anxiety. But how do you know what's coming from the heart and not your ego? Solutions that come from the heart should be of help to all parties involved. The solution should not serve one while harming another. And in case you think this means you must stay with your partner no matter what—even if she refuses treatment and behaves badly—this is not so. Sometimes you can unwittingly encourage, that is, *enable*, behavior that is harmful to the sufferer. In fact, if you were to leave such a partner for a spell, perhaps she would take action toward confronting the PTSD. Your loved one may realize that, without you there to help, treatment is the only road to survival.

Irrational Belief #5: The World Should Treat Me Fairly

Do you believe that life should be fair, particularly if you've always done those things your parents and authority figures told you were right? It's possible to become angry and embittered when things don't go as you wanted or planned—especially when you've always sought to take the higher path. But do you realize that sometimes those events that seem unfair at the time actually come to facilitate your greatest personal growth? Because many Americans are confused about what makes a person feel good for the long run, they do whatever it takes to avoid any problem at hand. However, some suggest that life comes to have more meaning when you grow mentally and spiritually through the problem-solving process. If something goes wrong or you don't feel that something is fair, you need to figure out a way to think about it in a more positive light, work through it, and grow because of it.

Again, because a person may lack this wisdom, he may seek to avoid the legitimate suffering problems can bring, stop growing mentally and spiritually, and actually come to experience greater pain from avoiding the problem than he would have if he'd just gone ahead and tackled it in the first place. Perhaps you've been observing this with your partner.

Is she using alcohol or drugs to self-medicate and feel better? Under the influence of chemicals, it's possible to ignore the realities of life and escape its pain—at least for a while. If your partner develops a tolerance for a drug, though, she might eventually be unable to attain the same relief found early on—even as she takes higher dosages of the substance. The day will likely come when she realizes this once best friend has turned on her and she may proceed to take life-threatening dosages of the drug.

It is best to awaken to the problems—fair or not—that life brings. Ask not how you could avoid a problem, but how you can best embrace and solve it instead. As you step forward to face your problems, take note of what you're learning along the way. You may learn any number of things about yourself, your partner, and your relationship. Observe it all. Then, after doing so, you may ask, in meditation or perhaps in your journal, *What am I to do with what I have learned from this experience?*

When you stop to think about all you've learned and how you've grown, perhaps you'll realize that by embracing what at the time seemed so unfair, you actually came to experience the grandest sense of who you are—or who you could become. Isn't there something wondrous and exciting about that? Remember, almost anyone can handle the good times. The tough times make the grandest statement about who you are.

Irrational Belief #6: Some People Are Bad and Must Be Punished

While you may know someone who operates under the belief that when someone does something that she views as bad, she should punish that person, here we're talking about the belief that a person is inherently bad and needs to be punished. For example, perhaps your partner is a wounded soldier who marched into Iraq because the United States had a goal to punish the "bad" Saddam Hussein and his regime while also rescuing the Iraqi people from this "evil" dictator. However, he and other military members unintentionally became the perpetrators of death and suffering instead. Your partner learned firsthand that the majority of people killed in a war zone are not "bad" people, but innocent civilians.

War veterans come to understand something that many of the rest of us do not. We want to believe that there are perpetrators, victims, and rescuers—and each group will forever play the same role in which they start out. However, whether someone jumps onto this triangle in his personal life or in the arena of war, he will likely discover that the role he plays can suddenly change. One day the soldier in Iraq is the rescuer of the people from an oppressive regime—just as he counted on being. But then, one day he realizes that, to the people he has been trying to rescue, he is perceived as the perpetrator. Indeed, they perceive themselves as his victims. Forced against his will into a role he had never intended to play, the war veteran might come to label himself as a "bad" person.

Can you now see how it is not always clear cut as to who is "good" and who is "bad," and why operating under this belief can prove troublesome? Particularly, though, if either you or your partner is applying this label to the self or the other, it's time to let go of this irrational belief. Only then will you find the ability to forgive.

Irrational Belief #7: It's Awful or Terrible When Things Don't Turn Out as I'd Like

It's basically impossible to enjoy or benefit from what's happening in the present when you adhere to this belief. You're too busy feeling sad or angry that things aren't as they should be—the way you wanted them to be, that is. And yet, who's to say that what you intended was actually the best way for things to unfold? Perhaps if you'd sit back and relax, and then flow with whatever has come to pass instead of bemoaning it, you'd be pleasantly surprised with what life ultimately delivers. Have you ever heard the saying that everything that happens is for your highest good?

Of course, this doesn't mean that life will be all fun and games. That may be what you'd prefer, but that isn't really what's for your highest good. As you've undoubtedly been discovering through your PTSD-impacted relationship, life presents challenges and problems. Perhaps you can think of them as opportunities for personal and spiritual growth.

The rough spots in the road may propel you forward on your own unique life path or mission. And who is to say that what you're experiencing right now may not be the most difficult thing you'll ever experience? Once you get beyond all this, you may find that the remainder of the journey is actually joyous. Can you hold on to this thought rather than allowing yourself to linger in that place where you are almost guaranteed to disintegrate into further misery? Remember, when you're thinking thoughts that feed either sadness or anger, you're likely to generate even more negative thoughts that will only take you further on that downward spiral. But you have a choice. You can think differently so you can feel differently. And when you feel differently, you are apt to behave differently, too.

Certainly, you may find your current situation quite challenging. That's understandable. It's not easy to switch from being an equal partner in a relationship to becoming the caregiver of someone with PTSD. In fact, this might seem awful or terrible. Certainly, it's okay to bemoan your fate for a little while. Nevertheless, if you hold on to this irrational belief, you may lose the ability to listen to your heart and take the right actions it may recommend for you. You may become increasingly angry instead, which will create even more stress for your PTSD-impacted partner—whose symptoms will then likely worsen. At that point, your relationship and your life will only deteriorate further. You don't want that, do you?

Let go of the idea that unless things always unfold as you envisioned, you'll become emotionally upset as a result. By letting this go, you open yourself up to new possibilities. You may even reach the point where you can take any experience and find something good about it. Maybe it helped you become a stronger person or you are now better able to empathize with others, for example. As a result, you should find yourself experiencing more acceptance and inner peace.

Irrational Belief #8: I Can't Change My Behavior or Take Any Kind of Corrective Action Unless I'm Upset

Are you afraid you won't act if you don't somehow get yourself all upset and angry? If that's the case, stop and remind yourself that extreme emotion often sabotages, undermines, or actually destroys your chances of getting the very things you claim you desire.

Let's say you had to take on a new job that affords the household a higher income because of your partner's inability to work as he once did. This has taken you outside of your comfort zone and, as a result, you've been struggling at this job. You've been making mistakes and perhaps even telling yourself that you're stupid and worthless because you keep making these mistakes. Instead of beating yourself up, try feeding yourself affirmations—statements in which you profess yourself already doing the thing you'd prefer you were doing. Start these statements with the words "I am." Some examples include:

- I am learning the new skills I need quickly and easily.
- I am experiencing joy and contentment while learning everything my job requires.
- I am competent and confident in my new job.

It's important to think this way because your mind perceives your self-talk as requests for how you want things to be. Such talk will likely help you bring forth more of those things you've been thinking about.

It's important to realize that being upset and having performance anxiety are not identical. Some performance anxiety can be helpful because it may motivate you to study harder or practice more—so your performance will likely improve. But if your anxiety level shoots up too high, you'll start feeding yourself negative thoughts. As a result, you might create the very things you didn't want. When you become upset, you lose your ability to focus or concentrate and the things you tackle are apt to be full of mistakes. Also, if you allow yourself to become very angry with another— even at God—you won't be capable of rational thinking. Yet, in that aroused state, you're likely to wrongly believe that you're taking constructive action. You'll undoubtedly come up with your most creative ideas or your best solutions when you're calm, which will in turn benefit your partner with PTSD.

Irrational Belief #9: I Shouldn't Have to Give Up Any Substance or Activity That Gives Me Pleasure Despite Its Potential Harm

This irrational belief promotes self-destructive behaviors that feel good because they medicate or suppress uncomfortable feelings. Although your partner may escape his painful feelings in such ways, please don't use things like food, alcohol, sex, shopping, etc. to squelch your own. By doing so, you're disregarding not only your feelings but also those underlying issues that caused those feelings to arise in the first place. Instead, think of emotional pain as delivering an important message that you ignore at your own peril. Remember, if you allow yourself to experience these emotions, you may become more inclined to step onto a path of healing. Allow this alert system to work—to awaken you to the unfinished emotional business you must attend to.

Initially, it may be more painful to cope with your issues than to escape through substance abuse, but, as we've already discussed, relying on substances or behaviors that make you feel good in the moment will be destructive to your health and well-being in the long run. It may be necessary to withstand a dark night of the soul to ultimately emerge from your current experiences as a transformed person. The good news? As a transformed person, you'll likely unearth an authentic self that isn't addicted to feeling good. By finding this authentic self, you're more apt to experience contentment—no matter your current life circumstances.

Irrational Belief # 10: I Have No Ability to Control My Emotions Because Everything I Experience Is Externally Caused

Hopefully, you understand that this belief isn't true. However, you may feel that your life is out of control because of your partner's PTSD. Consider the fact that one way to gain more control over your life is to drop this belief and instead work to change your thinking.

The PTSD sufferer's brain reacts to certain familiar patterns with an immediate freeze, fight, or flight reaction. This automatic response kicks in before the more rational part of the brain can evaluate the situation and decide if such a response is justified. While the PTSD sufferer may start to explode because of her brain chemistry, in most cases, she can be taught to recognize and stop the explosion by using that rational part of the brain to think new thoughts. If your partner can learn to change her PTSD-impacted brain, don't you suspect you could do the same? Get started by letting go of this belief.

Irrational Belief # 11: My Past History Determines My Present Behavior and I Have No Control Over It

Your history can profoundly affect who you are and how you behave. If you had a traumatic childhood and have refused to examine your past and how it drives you today, it will likely have an ongoing negative hold on your life. However, the brain is not permanently wired to be one way and thus unable to change. Instead, it has plasticity—something we didn't know even a couple of decades ago. Indeed, medications and psychotherapy change the brain. SSRIs cause neurogenesis—whereby the brain grows new neurons. Also, neurons form new connections as a result of cognitive behavioral therapy.

Still, while there is hope of change, some people would rather blame their pasts for their current lifestyles and behaviors, rather than take on the pain and hard work of making changes. In blaming and failing to change, however, they forsake an opportunity for true happiness and serenity.

It will be more challenging for your partner to change than for the average person, but it will be easier and the results superior if help is sought early on—within months of PTSD's onset. Nevertheless, even PTSD sufferers who are Vietnam War veterans have been helped by therapeutic approaches implemented some twenty years after they developed PTSD symptoms. So please, realize that your partner doesn't need to be a victim of the past—or of that trauma he experienced. Believe this, and help your loved one believe this as well.

If you have your own issues, get into therapy and start working on them. Don't be surprised if you see some issues that you ignored before come to light. Changes in your relationship may bring these issues to the forefront. Accepting that you may have your own work to do that will further your personal growth or spiritual development may help you see that your life isn't all about your partner and his problems. Embrace the need to change, realize that change is possible, and remember that when you stop changing, you start dying. Choose life instead.

Irrational Belief # 12: The Beliefs I Learned as a Child Can Guide Me Through Adulthood

As a child, adults handed you beliefs that defined how you experienced yourself; you had little choice or control over the beliefs that would guide your life. Today, you need beliefs that match with what you want for your relationship and your future life—beliefs that allow your thinking and behavior to align. Otherwise, you'll likely experience ongoing anxiety and depression.

Do you have hand-me-down beliefs from childhood that aren't a match for the way you want to behave or be today? You may be aware of some of these, but you may also be operating on others that lie outside of your level of awareness. If you're experiencing anxiety or feeling depressed regularly, this may be a clue that your behavior and beliefs aren't in alignment. Try the following exercise to figure out what hand-me-down beliefs you hold.

EXERCISE BECOMING AWARE OF PROBLEMATIC HAND-ME-DOWN BELIEFS

How do you become more aware of the problematic hand-me-down beliefs that may be creating problems? Begin by thinking of areas where you're having problems today. Perhaps you believe that you're not acting compassionately enough toward your partner. Maybe you're having trouble with financial matters—either the actual money management or just the idea that you have to assume the responsibility for earning the money the family needs.

On one sheet of paper, write down one of these issues along with short descriptive notes—or expanded comments if you prefer. There is no right or wrong way to do this. Then, on another sheet of paper, write down another problematic area. Don't limit yourself as to the number of problems, but do limit yourself to one problem area per sheet of paper.

1. Pick up one of those sheets of paper and write down everything you can remember your parents and/or authority figures telling you about that problematic area. Perhaps nothing was said, but a parent behaved in a way that made a strong statement and caused you to develop a certain belief. Write that down as well. For example, if you believe that you're not as compassionate toward your partner as you should be, could this stem from the fact that you watched your mother deny all of her desires while she tended solely to those of your father? Write this down. ➤

2. After you have done this for each of the issues identified on the separate sheets of paper, make a list of
the beliefs you suspect you adopted from hearing or
observing the things that you did. Leave a few lines
between each belief so you can come back later and
write something further regarding each belief.

3. Go back through the sheets of paper and look at
the beliefs on each. Star any that you want to continue to hold—that still support who you are today or
the person you are yet striving to become. Place the
papers with starred beliefs in one pile.

4. Take the pile with starred beliefs. Work through them
one sheet at a time. In the space below the starred
belief, write down a behavior that you could engage
in that supports or demonstrates that belief.

5. Study the beliefs that you didn't star that could be
getting in your way today. What could you think instead—what belief could you adopt that may serve
you better than the one you were handed down?
For example, rather than believing that you need to
totally sacrifice your own needs and desires for the
sake of your partner, you could write a new belief
such as: *I always strive to maintain a healthy balance
between the needs of my partner and what I need
and desire to have a healthy and productive life. I
do this by* (state some things you intend to do in the
future to put this new belief into play). Write this in
the space below the handed-down belief that is dysfunctional for your adult life.

6. Write out or type out a list of what you seek to believe and act upon in the present. You might keep this
in your personal journal notebook or in a picture ➤

frame. Review these beliefs periodically to ensure that they're still serving you well. Feel free to change any as the need arises.

Always remember that beliefs need not be fixed. You can change yours whenever it would serve you to do so—such as when there isn't a match between your beliefs and your behavior on an ongoing basis. You may experience guilt when you initially realize that your beliefs and behavior aren't in alignment. The good news? You'll probably be motivated to explore what isn't working and what needs to be changed. ■

Of course, sometimes life demands that you behave in ways inconsistent with your beliefs. In fact, your partner may be experiencing guilt because he behaved in ways inconsistent with his personal beliefs during the course of the PTSD-producing trauma. In such a case, it is best for the individual to stop beating up on himself—to let go of his guilt and adopt a belief in forgiveness instead.

People experience psychological distress when there is not a match between their behavior and their beliefs. You alleviate this distress by either changing how you think about something or how you behave. What you do is up to you, but it is important to realize that your beliefs serve as a filter. You can't fully take in all you are exposed to or experience over the course of a day. Therefore, your beliefs guide you as to what to attend to and what to disregard. This is why beliefs influence perception. Then your perceptions influence how you experience your world and your life. In turn, your experiences influence what you believe. Experiences may prove or disprove the beliefs you were already holding. After you experience new things, you may come to hold new beliefs. This is perfectly okay. Remember, changing and growing is good.

Both you and your partner may have quite a job before you with regard to your beliefs. You may both face tough and emotionally painful times as you examine them. Perhaps you'll come to realize that there was nothing wrong with the underlying belief, but the way you had to act upon it didn't work out as you had envisioned. Things likely happened outside your control. Circumstances changed. In your case, you may still cling to the belief that you should be a supportive partner through sickness and in health. Nevertheless, if you realize that your partner isn't taking action to deal with the PTSD and its destructive symptoms, you may not be able to do this. You can't toss your life away for another who is intent on not making any attempt to change.

Remember, tomorrow offers you a chance for a fresh start. Don't let past mistakes—or the fact that you've clung to any of these twelve irrational beliefs—overwhelm you. Rather, step forward on that pathway toward change. Seize this opportunity to change your relationship—whether it be for your partner, for your self, or for your life—by changing how you think.

Chapter 9

Tools for a Better Relationship

155 Questions to Ask

156 Calling a Time-Out

158 Active or Reflective Listening

163 Speaker/Listener Technique

164 The Art of Correction

168 Underlying Conflict

173 Great Expectations?

179 Problem Solving

182 Final Comments

All relationships experience conflict, but when PTSD is in the picture, conflicts need to be handled very carefully. Remember, you want to ensure there's not undue stress for your PTSD sufferer, since stress may well cause your loved one's symptoms to worsen—and your relationship to further deteriorate. Let's look at more skills to add to your toolbelt that will help you deal with conflict in your relationship in constructive ways.

As we begin, be aware that your partner may not be able to participate in some of these processes as a person without a mental health issue could. Also, because PTSD cases vary from simple to complex, it's difficult to suggest what your partner may be capable—or incapable—of doing. Thus, proceed carefully. Expect the best, but always be prepared for the worst.

If your partner's response leaves much to be desired, become indignant with the PTSD—not with your partner. Don't take this personally or assume your partner is intentionally being uncooperative. Then again, don't assume that your loved one will always continue to function at the same level that he might when you first try to engage him in these activities. For example, perhaps your partner is incapable of participating in problem solving in the beginning and, as a result, you continue to take it upon yourself to handle everything. Down the road, give your loved one another opportunity to try this again with you and the family. Always hold out hope that things will get better.

If your partner fails to make the type of progress you had anticipated, try to hide your disappointment, and then hold back on making demands. Your partner is likely finding his inabilities as frustrating as you are. While the PTSD has likely impacted your partner's memory and thinking ability, he undoubtedly is aware of many of the functional declines he has experienced. He likely faces losses even more bitter than yours. If you remain sensitive to this fact, you should find it easier to remain involved with your loved one in healthy ways, while backing off when interaction become too stressful for him.

It may help to think of what you're doing as similar to a single-participant research design, where a researcher tracks the changes created by a specific therapeutic intervention on an individual's behavior. You could track how your partner responds to the various processes in which you try to engage him. In doing so, you may notice that certain activities or approaches work better than others—that some are too stressful while others seem manageable. Focus on the latter until your partner shows further improvement from treatment. Then, give some of the others a try again.

Certainly, dealing with your partner with PTSD may at times seem more like interacting with a small child or an elderly person than a normal adult. You must lower your expectations as to the level of performance you can expect from your loved one. You'll also want to be prepared to celebrate even seemingly minor changes as great strides because both your partner and you will likely feel better and benefit from doing so. It should help keep that fire of hope still burning

Questions to Ask

Have you ever tried to vent to a friend about a problem, only to have the person launch into a discussion regarding how you should solve it? You may have been displeased with your friend's response. Well, remember this when it comes to your partner with PTSD. Sometimes when you mean to be supportive, you could be acting in ways that actually annoy your partner.

So, instead of marching forth and doing what you suspect needs to be done, ask your partner some screening questions first. Here are some questions to ask:

- Do you need a hug (or some other sign of support)?
- Do you need to vent about what's going on and just have me listen?
- Do you need to be left alone?
- Do you want me to offer my take on things or give advice?

Hopefully, your loved one will provide a useful reply that gives you direction on how to proceed. If that doesn't happen, and your partner ignores you or becomes angry instead, back down—at least for now. Plan to try this approach another time. Also, don't act shocked or say anything if your partner later agrees to participate, other than to perhaps offer a positive comment about how this shows the progress she has been making through treatment.

Calling a Time-Out

If you're going to talk about a problem and flush out solutions, you and your partner may need to make use of a technique that here, as in sports, is called a time-out. This technique proves helpful when a couple starts discussing a problem but one or both of them become too upset to talk about the situation rationally. Since no real progress can be made under such circumstances—but hurtful things might be said that could further damage the relationship already harmed by PTSD—it's important to call a time-out. Here are some further points about time-outs that should help you implement this technique:

- It doesn't matter who calls the time-out. However, since yours is not a normal relationship now, and your partner might be suffering from myriad problems that may cause her to become irritated or anxious, and yet she might fail to call a time-out when in such an aroused state, you should be prepared to take this action.
- When you call a time-out, both verbally express what you are doing and make the t-sign as is used at sporting events.
- Both of you need to honor a time-out whenever one is called. Plan to immediately separate without any further discussion of the current issue—or about the need for a time-out itself. You should plan to leave the room and go elsewhere after you call the time-out.
- Neither party should use a time-out as a means of avoiding talking about a certain problem or topic. There should be the understanding between the two of you that you will always get back together to discuss the topic again. You might have a general rule that you will try to come back together a couple of hours later, try again the next day, or something along those lines.
- When you get back together to discuss the topic, if one person is still too upset to have this discussion, call another time-out, but also try to set a time to have this discussion again.

- If your partner is abusing substances and is rarely sober, it may be nearly impossible to ever meet and have a rational discussion. Nevertheless, if you know that your partner tends to be sober in the morning but not later in the day, then after you call a time-out, try to always establish that best time as when you'll come back together.
- If it is becoming difficult to get something discussed that you initially brought to the table, reconsider how important the issue is. Can it be dropped? Can you handle whatever it is without your partner's involvement? Can you generate solutions with the help of a friend, parent, sibling, etc. instead? Could your partner's therapist help you decide how to deal with what you face instead of expecting your PTSD-impacted partner to do so?

Your partner may well want to discuss subjects with you that she finds difficult to cover without becoming upset because of the PTSD. Hopefully, using this time-out technique will help the two of you have success. Even if you never needed something like this before, realize that things are different now. Give it a try.

Active or Reflective Listening

Let's look at a technique that you and your partner can use to ensure that you're listening to each other. Active or reflective listening is designed both to help you better listen to each other and to ensure that you understand what the other is saying and feeling. When using this technique, you essentially repeat back what your partner has just said, putting it into your own words. You can also take a stab at identifying the feeling that you suspect your partner is experiencing even if it wasn't specifically stated.

As before, this technique may work for the two of you as it's presented. Then again, you may need to make modifications. You may also decide that this technique won't improve matters until your partner has further treatment. If that's the case, don't forget about this technique indefinitely. Give it another try later on.

-------------------- CASE STUDY --------------------

James and Sandy

Your partner may or may not express a feeling in what he says, but it could well be implied. In such a case, you can parrot back what your loved one said and express what you imagine he is feeling—after trying to put yourself in your partner's shoes. Let's see how this works when Sandy actively listens to her husband, James, who suffers from PTSD.

James: *I really don't want to go to that event tonight. I might embarrass myself.*

Sandy: *You don't want to go because you're afraid you might do something that will make people stare?*

Having expressed how you think your partner is feeling, allow him to tell you if you got the feeling right or not.

James: *I just don't want to go to this event—just like I didn't want to go last week. Remember how you asked me to go to that concert with you? Can't you get it through your head I don't like to be in crowds—because something might happen?*

Sandy: *Do I hear you saying I shouldn't keep asking you to these events because you don't want to go to any of them? And is it because you're afraid you might do something that would prove embarrassing?*

James: *I might have a flashback. Then what are you going to do? Neither of us needs that.*

Sandy: *I see your point. I'll stop asking you to go to anything—at least until you and your therapist get your PTSD symptoms under better control.*

It may seem strange at first to try to put something your partner just said into your own words, but while it may seem uncomfortable or awkward, using active listening accomplishes a couple of significant things. It first helps to make sure you heard your partner correctly, rather than simply assuming you did and then acting on an incorrect assumption. Also, your partner may be thinking aloud when he talks. As a result, he may not be clear as to what he believes or means until he hears his own words spoken aloud. When you feed back what your partner said, he may suddenly realize that he doesn't actually believe the words he just spoke.

Because of this latter possibility, don't assume that because your partner corrects you after you've given your feedback, you heard him incorrectly. Remember, your loved one may have gained further clarity as to his own thinking just by hearing you speak his words. So, to ensure you heard this revised message correctly, just feed back what your partner had to say this second time around. Don't point out how inconsistent he is being, or say anything else negative. Simply try to understand your partner's thoughts and emotions—and help him understand them as well.

────────────── CASE STUDY ──────────────

Leo and Anna

To see how this could play out, let's look at a more extended example. It involves Leo, a man who has struggled with PTSD/SUD, and his wife, Anna.

Leo: *You won't believe what happened today. I was finally ready to try to go to an A.A. meeting and the car wouldn't start.*

Anna: *That must have been very frustrating for you. I know it took some real effort to get yourself mentally ready to head to that first A.A. meeting.*

Leo: *I guess it was frustrating—more so than I realized at the time. Maybe that's why I got so angry when this happened.*

Anna: *You got all worked up when the car wouldn't start?*

Leo: *I didn't realize how angry I was until I got back into the house, walked straight for the refrigerator, and started to search for a beer. Of course, I couldn't find one.*

Anna: *So, does that mean you're glad I decided not to keep beer in the house anymore for anyone, even though you said it wouldn't matter if I did—that it would never tempt you?*

Leo: *Yeah, I was actually relieved there wasn't anything in this house to drink.*

Anna: *All's well that ends well.*

Leo: *I guess I need A.A. more than I thought I did.*

Anna: *So, are you saying that now you're ready to go to A.A. whereas before, you weren't so committed?*

Leo: *Maybe it's a good thing that things unfolded this way, you think?*

Anna: *It sounds like you have a renewed commitment to this part of your treatment plan.*

Leo: *I guess I do.*

As you review this case study, can you see that there was a positive outcome from Anna's willingness to engage in active listening with Leo? They both came to realize that Leo is actually committed now to going to A.A. when that wasn't obvious before. Another wife without Anna's skills and desire to use active listening might have gotten sidetracked and made some disparaging remark when Leo made the comment about trying to find a beer, for instance. She may have ended up angry at her partner rather than feeling positive and hopeful as Anna likely did at the end of this discussion.

Speaker/Listener Technique

This is another technique that can help couples communicate about a sensitive or tough issue where both parties want to be heard. It's structured and has rules—some for the speaker, others for the listener. However, each person plays each role—and is allowed to speak as often as needed—until both parties feel the issue has been properly discussed. Here are the rules:

- The designated speaker has the floor until she is ready to give it up—but the speaker must give the listener a chance to respond at some point.
- Use an object to indicate who has the floor—to designate the speaker. For example, toss a stuffed animal back and forth. Whoever is holding the stuffed animal is the speaker while the other must listen. When the speaker tosses the stuffed animal back to the listener, it is time to reverse roles.
- The speaker should pause regularly. At these times, the listener should use active or reflective listening to ensure he understood the speaker correctly as well as to remain focused. Also, it's acceptable for the listener to ask the speaker to further explain something. However, the listener should not make remarks about what the speaker has said. These comments should be held in mind, and then spoken when the listener has become the speaker.
- Stick to one topic or problem while using this technique.
- Don't dig up dirt from the past—remain in the present.

- Concentrate on voicing thoughts and feelings through-out this process rather than moving into problem-solving mode. Keep doing this until you both believe that the other has heard everything you wanted to say.
- Gently confront the other person if she gets off task. Don't condemn her for doing this—simply get back on track together as quickly as possible.
- Call a time-out if things start getting out of hand—and then adhere to the rules you've established for time-outs.

Remember, when using this approach, you should not expect to have the problem resolved at the end of the process. This technique is a means for you both to get your thoughts and feelings out there about an issue so that each of you knows where the other stands. Again, your partner with PTSD may or may not be up to using this technique, but you might as well give it a try.

The Art of Correction

This is a technique you can use to try to point out something your partner is doing that you'd prefer he didn't, and to offer up a solution that you'd like to see him implement instead. However, before you get too excited and want to start diplomatically correcting every last thing your partner does that you don't like, realize that doing so would likely overwhelm him. Select your battles carefully. Furthermore, you may want to practice the technique with your partner on a less complicated and relatively unimportant issue before trying something of mega-importance to you.

Before delving into the steps to correcting someone diplomatically, it's important to remind yourself that everything the person does is not annoying or problematic. Keep this in mind as you go on to describe the behavior you don't like and how it could be changed to better please you. Since the process involves a few more steps than this, they are all listed and described below.

1. **Positive affirmation:** Tell your partner something that you liked about his behavior at the time of the action or incident you intend to correct diplomatically. If you can't come up with anything, think about something positive that has generally been true in the past that is somehow related to what you are about to correct.

2. **Three-part assertion:** Make a three-part assertion in which you tell your partner what he did that you didn't like, how it made you feel, and why.

3. **Description of the preferred behavior or solution:** Suggest to your partner something he could do instead that you would like.

4. **Why implementing this solution will be rewarding:** Give a reason as to why this suggested change may work better for the two of you.

5. **Offer of incentive:** Offer an incentive or payoff to your partner for trying your suggestion.

6. **Request for approval:** Ask for your partner's agreement to try your suggestion.

Be aware that, despite the fact that you are trying to take a gentle approach to correcting your partner, he may still not handle your criticism well. If your partner cannot cope with this process, call a time-out. While the break may end up being temporary, you also could decide that it's best to drop the issue, at least until your partner has had further treatment.

――――――――― CASE STUDY ―――――――――

Ellie and Martin

Let's look at an example of how this process might be implemented. Here, Ellie corrects her PTSD-suffering husband, Martin, diplomatically.

I'm glad you went to the show today with the kids and me. It felt good to be a family again. **(Positive affirmation)**

When you gave Robbie the drink and expected him to carry it into the theater, I felt anxious because I realized he was apt to spill it—just as he did. **(Three-part assertion)**

How about the next time we go to the theater with the kids, you carry his drink into the show, and then he can handle it after he's seated. **(Description of the preferred behavior or solution)**

This way neither of us has to be embarrassed or feel bad because Robbie created extra work for the theater employees. **(Why implementing this solution will be rewarding)**

If you'll grab his drink the next time, I'll go ahead and pay. **(Offer of incentive)** Would this work for you? **(Request for approval or agreement)**

————————— CASE STUDY —————————

Tom and Suzy

Here is an example of Tom, correcting his PTSD-suffering wife, Suzy, diplomatically.

I like the way you've been making a real effort to talk with me in recent days. It feels good to be connected again. **(Positive affirmation)**

When you brushed me off over lunch, though, it made me feel anxious because I instantly thought this PTSD symptom was back, and that you'd soon slip into full-fledged avoidance again. **(Three-part assertion)**

How about the next time I feel you may be blowing me off because the PTSD is talking again, that I bring this to your attention? Then I'll ask you if you're having a tough time of it and, if you are, I'll suggest we set a time to talk later. **(Description of the preferred behavior or solution)**

This way, you get the space you need in the moment, but without me feeling increasingly resentful because suddenly everything seems to be all about you. **(Why implementing this solution will be rewarding)**

If you'll do this, I'll make a concerted effort to take out the garbage every night like you want me to—without having to be asked time and again. **(Offer of incentive)**

Are you okay with this? **(Request for approval or agreement)**

Underlying Conflict

While many people prefer to avoid conflict and allow problems to fester, some seek to solve them too soon. In fact, they end up trying to resolve the wrong issues. No wonder they come up with solutions that often fail dismally. To help ensure that this doesn't happen to you and your partner, it's important that you have what will perhaps be a new framework for looking at your relationship conflicts. You'll want to work through this before you move on to the next skill, problem solving.

Most couples start fighting over an event—something that is happening in the moment in their day-to-day life. But so often, there is anger or pain from an unresolved issue that causes one party to explode about something that to an outside observer might have seemed fairly insignificant. As long as the issue remains unresolved, such conflicts are likely to erupt time and again.

The major issues that affect most partners are money, sex, and communication. Other common issues include in-laws, children, recreation, use of chemical substances, religion, career demands, and housework. Hidden issues that create problems in relationships include such things as power, caring, recognition, commitment, integrity, and acceptance.

You realize that the presence of PTSD in your relationship has made some of the issues you were already dealing with worse than ever. For example, the presence of PTSD has likely created more financial strain. It may have resulted in the demise of your sex life. And since your partner is likely exhibiting avoidance, you're probably experiencing more limited communication and interaction with him than you'd prefer. You may also have issues regarding how your partner treats the children—perhaps because he blows up at them, is verbally abusive, or essentially ignores them. Of course, if your partner uses chemical substances to try to keep PTSD symptoms at bay, you may fight about this. Furthermore, are you displeased that you now have to essentially run the household single-handedly on top of everything else you must deal with? Indeed, as if there weren't enough issues for you to cope with as a couple before, PTSD has likely made matters only more overwhelming.

At this point, we need to talk about another concept, that of positions. Your position represents the concrete things you say you want. For example, you may be looking for a new job since your partner developed PTSD. You tell potential employers that you must have an income of so many thousand dollars a year. However, you have reasons for holding to your position—it is not arbitrary. Those things that underlie your position are your interests.

Interests are intangible motivations that lead you to hold to a certain position. Therefore, your needs, wants, concerns, and fears can all determine your interests. For example, when you state your position that you must make so many thousand dollars per year, you may do so because you have an interest—to be able to meet your family's living expenses and save money for a financial cushion—and this dollar amount allows you to do that.

Does your partner share your interest? Let's assume he is not as worried about meeting living expenses as you are. As a result, when you tell him you declined a job you'd been excited about because the salary wasn't high enough, he is upset. He professes it was the perfect job for you. You respond and tell him about another job you're thinking of taking instead. After all, it meets your position. Your husband picks up on your lack of enthusiasm. He suggests that there may be a way to take the job that you'd prefer and still meet your interest—but you'll have to back off your position. You don't see how that could ever be possible. He suggests the two of you look at ways to cut expenses so you can have the job you desire and still develop the financial cushion you need to feel safe.

Here are some additional points to ponder:

- In conflict resolution, your goal should be to develop a win-win solution rather than allowing one person to win by getting his position met while the other walks away disappointed or resentful. After all, this undermines the relationship, while you want to build it instead.

- Often parties in conflict cannot both obtain their positions, but they can have their underlying interests met instead. However, each person must back off of his position to accomplish this. If you'll come to the table ready to discover new ways to meet your interests, you may find that this conflict is resolved once and for all.

- You usually won't have your own interests satisfied unless you seek to understand and deal with the interests of your partner (or any other person with whom you're in conflict) as well.

- You may think you know what your interest is behind your position when you actually do not. So, to get at it, ask yourself why you want something or what problem you're trying to solve by sticking to a certain position. But don't accept your immediate response. Instead, ask yourself why you're holding to that interest. For example, you may realize that you've been holding out for a certain salary to pay for a current lifestyle that has been defined more by neighborhood pressure than what your family actually needs to sustain itself.

- Realize that you and your partner are probably arguing over events—such as the fact that your partner didn't attend the children's school concert or wouldn't have sex with you the night before. Don't keep fighting about these smaller problems, but dig deeper to get at the underlying issues. As you strive to do this, realize that some of the events you argue about may stem from your partner's PTSD symptoms. If your partner gets treatment for PTSD, this may take care of some of these events. For example, his unwillingness to do things with you would decrease because the symptom of avoidance would be gone. Then again, there may be events that you've fought about since before PTSD entered the picture. Seek to understand the issues lying beneath these.
- To accomplish win-win solutions, it's important to accept ownership of the problem. If you have trouble doing this, remind yourself that if you didn't have a position to begin with, there would be nothing to argue about. You would just concede to your partner.
- Realize that too often people spend more time arguing about who is most responsible for the current problem than figuring out what can be done to resolve or improve matters. Avoid doing this. After all, when you have a partner with PTSD, it is easy to lay blame. Remind yourself that your partner didn't ask to develop PTSD. He probably dislikes having it as much as you would dislike becoming blind as the result of an accident. So stay focused on how you can create wins for the two of you despite the obstacles that PTSD has dragged forth.

- Consider how to facilitate a healing environment for your partner's PTSD while developing a solution that meets your common interests. For example, if your partner is currently incapable of connecting with you by going to see a movie in a crowded theater but you've been insisting she do this, back off your position. Ask her if she would be interested in connecting in some other way. Perhaps she'll indicate that she would be happy to have you rent the desired movie when it comes out on DVD, and to watch it together in the quiet of your home.

Now that you have an understanding of the concepts relevant to the negotiation process, let's look at how you would put it all together to resolve some of your own conflicts as a couple.

--------------------- CASE STUDY ---------------------

Liz and Trevor

Let's examine a scenario that involves a PTSD-impacted couple resolving their conflict through negotiation. This case study involves Liz and her husband, Trevor, who has PTSD.

Liz's Position: *Liz wants Trevor to help out more with household chores since he isn't working full-time anymore, whereas she is.*

Trevor's Position: *Trevor only wants to engage in activities that can help him alleviate or better manage his PTSD symptoms.*

Liz's Interests: *Liz wants more free time on weekends to go out and have fun with the family instead of having to remain at home to do chores she couldn't complete during the workweek.*

Trevor's Interests: *Trevor doesn't want to do anything that might create stress. He's fearful the stress will worsen his PTSD symptoms or trigger a flashback.*

When you examine the interests of Liz and Trevor, isn't it obvious that, while they're in conflict because they're sticking to their positions, they could probably come up with a solution that meets both of their interests? You could state their common interest as this: Both Liz and Trevor want to engage in more activities in their lives that help minimize stress, while at the same time they want to avoid or minimize the number of activities that are stressful. Once Liz and Trevor are aware they have a common interest, they can move toward fulfilling it.

To reach a solution, Liz and Trevor could write out a goal or an intention statement such as: Our intention is to have more fun and less stress in our lives, but we need to do this in a way such that neither of us feels overwhelmed or burdened by the tasks necessary to maintain the household.

Great Expectations?

Expectations are beliefs you hold about how things should be, either currently or in the future. Feelings of disappointment, sadness, or anger can arise when your expectations are not met. Your expectations—which are often unreasonable—can create problems for you because they often remain outside your awareness; you don't realize how they're driving you. Moreover, even if your expectations are reasonable, they may remain unspoken. Therefore, unless your partner, family, and friends are excellent mind readers, these expectations are apt to go unmet.

Expectations may lie behind some of the positions and issues that you and your partner need to deal with as a couple. For example, you may be clinging to expectations that are reasonable for a relationship that hasn't been impacted by PTSD but are not reasonable for you and your partner today. To help you become more aware of your expectations, you may find the following exercise helpful.

EXERCISE ANALYZING CONFLICT AND PROBLEMATIC EXPECTATIONS

Take out twelve sheets of paper. Using the categories listed below in bold type, title each of the twelve sheets. Then list not just one expectation, but every expectation—as illustrated in the points below—that you can think of that falls under that title or category that may be creating problems within your relationship. Some of the categories may end up having a long list, while others may end up with nothing. Be as honest and forthright as possible. This is for your eyes only.

Money: My partner should make more money than I do; we should be able to purchase most everything that our friends have, as well as enjoy the same types of recreational activities and vacations; we should still save ➤

regularly toward college for the children—and at the same dollar amount as we did before.

Recreation: It's okay to do things apart during the week, but we should do most everything together on the weekend.

Communication: My partner should be willing to talk something over whenever I feel the need, even if he doesn't feel like it.

Friends: I should be able to go out with my girlfriends without being questioned as to where we're going; we should get together with other couples at least once a month like we did in the past; my partner needs to stop spending so much time with his war buddies and reconnect with his old friends instead.

Career or Employment: My husband needs to go back to work as soon as possible. In fact, this should be one of his treatment goals; my partner should take the highest paying job he's offered and learn how to live with the stress instead of using the PTSD as an excuse to do something less demanding.

In-Laws: My husband should be responsible for maintaining a relationship with his parents, not leave this for me to do.

Alcohol and Drugs: A wife should support her husband if he's striving to get better, including by going to Al-Anon and doing things he requests of her to promote his sobriety; a wife should keep the house free of any alcoholic beverages if her husband has had a drinking problem. ➤

Sex: My husband should initiate sex and not leave it to me all the time.

Children or Potential Children: Our children should be allowed to be children, not treated like little soldiers.

Religion: My husband and I should seek to grow together spiritually.

Household Tasks: My husband should be responsible for most household chores since he doesn't work full time as I do.

Other: None at this time.

Study each page and what you wrote. Have your expectations become positions to which you've been clinging? Were you aware of this fact before you wrote these things down? Even if these expectations haven't become positions, can you appreciate the need to be aware of them anyway—that they could get in the way of you and your partner having the type of relationship that you desire in the future?

Look at each expectation again, one by one. Decide if it is one you desire to keep or to let go of instead. Cross out those you believe you can readily give up.

Go back over those expectations you wish to keep. To discover why you cling to a given expectation, silently ask yourself why you have this expectation. Write that reason down beside or below the expectation. (You may want to ask "Why?" multiple times, not just once. After you write down your initial answer, ask yourself why you ➤

hold to whatever it is you wrote down. Keep doing this until you feel satisfied that you've gotten to the root of the matter.)

Study the reasons that you've listed. Do you spot anything that may be underlying those things you and your partner are in conflict about today? Place a check mark by any of these expectations.

Decide which of the expectations you've checked off have led to positions that you hold. Write down each of these positions.

Go through each position one by one. To get to the issue or issues behind each position, ask yourself why you have this position in the first place. Then write down all underlying issues for each position.

Prioritize these issues by their current importance to you. Then determine whether there are any high-priority items that you can somehow resolve or meet on your own. If it is necessary to involve your partner, try to pick out a low-priority item that you believe your partner will be able to handle to test-drive this process. If it goes well, you may then try a higher priority item that you suspect will still be manageable for your partner. Handle this with sensitivity. Realize that you may have to wait until your partner has undergone more treatment before you can use this process to carve out win-win solutions for the two of you. ∎

In case you're unclear as to how to deal with your expectations, take a look at the expectation listed under Recreation
in the listing of the twelve categories of typical problem areas
for couples: *It's okay to do things apart during the week, but we
should do most everything together on the weekend.* Let's assume
a woman, Jeanette, whose husband, Steve, has PTSD wrote
this expectation and it is one she wants to keep. Why may
this be so? Well, Jeanette may realize that a couple is more
likely to grow apart if they never do anything significant together that is fun. And in actuality, it is true that the couple
that plays together is more inclined to stay together. Having
fun with someone makes you more inclined to see that person
in a positive light than when all your interactions are about
problems. But is this something reasonable for Jeanette to
expect of Steve with his PTSD? Won't this create needless
stress for him? And won't that stress diminish the intent of
having fun?

This could indeed happen. Therefore, if this expectation
has become an issue for you as it has for Jeanette, you and
your partner may agree to engage in one significant activity together each weekend that he is comfortable doing. For
example, if your partner has indicated that, since developing the PTSD, he finds it less stressful to plan activities in
advance instead of being spontaneous as he was before, you
may agree to sit down at a certain time during the week,
study the community calendar, and come up with one event
you'd both enjoy that wouldn't be anxiety producing for
your partner.

When you're willing and able to examine your expectations
and see how they've been feeding your positions and issues, it
becomes easier to talk to your partner about areas of conflict,
back off from positions, take note of the similar issues you're

both striving to see met, and develop win-win solutions. Can you see that now?

While it is possible that you and your partner may actually come up with a solution to a problem you face as a couple through the process of clarifying your positions and interests, you also may need another tool known as problem solving. While there is a chance your partner won't be able to actively participate in problem solving because of his PTSD symptoms, you can still use this tool yourself to come up with win-win solutions that you can implement for the benefit of your relationship.

Problem Solving

Essentially, when problem solving you want to develop a solution that appears to meet the goal or the statement of intention that you and your partner developed. To accomplish this task, you must first brainstorm possible solutions that could fulfill or meet it.

When you engage in brainstorming, you and your partner will generate a list of ideas that can range from quite reasonable to far-fetched. It doesn't matter which type they are—just write down any idea no matter how crazy it may sound. After all, something crazy could lead to a more practical idea later on. By the way, write down all these ideas without discussing them first. While it is acceptable to ask for clarification of your partner's idea, that should be the extent of your discussion. In other words, the person presenting the idea says nothing to promote it, and the one hearing the idea for the first time makes no comments as to its worth or practicality.

When it gets to the point where neither one of you can think of any possibilities to add, go back and look at the practicality of each possible solution. Discuss the positives and negatives of every idea tossed out there. While you do this, keep in mind the issues each of you has that the solution is intended to meet. Write these pros and cons down for each potential solution. After this, select the one that looks the most beneficial and agree to try it for a certain amount of time. Of course, the amount of time you assign to it will vary depending upon the nature of the solution.

After you have tried a solution for that set amount of time, sit down together and evaluate how this solution has been working for both of you. If it has been good for one of you but not the other, try another solution from the list. Again, try it out for a specific period of time.

Hopefully, this second potential solution will work for the two of you. If it doesn't, don't be afraid to try another. Remember, when you have a partner suffering from PTSD, coming up with workable solutions to your relationship issues is going to be more challenging than for the average couple. Just try to maintain a positive attitude about it all. You may find it easier to do this if you approach the implementation of each potential solution as a noble experiment, or an adventure where you are bushwhacking your own trail through unknown territory—or use some other metaphor or image that helps keep your spirits high. And remember, considering the fact that your ultimate choice may impact your relationship for quite awhile, it's worth spending time to generate the right solution.

EXERCISE PROBLEM-SOLVING WORKSHEET

Goal or statement of intention: _____

My initial position (if applicable): _____

My partner's initial position (if applicable): _____

My interest(s): _____

My partner's interest(s): _____

Suggestions	Pros	Cons

We agree to try the checked solution starting _____
until _____, at which time we'll evaluate this solution.
We'll decide then to continue it, modify it, or try another
solution as needed.

Signed   Signed

_____   _____

Date   Date

_____   _____

Final Comments

Because you and your partner are individuals with your own needs and wants, there's bound to be conflict within your relationship anyway. However, because PTSD has turned this duo into a triad, you face new considerations that you didn't before—such as what's needed to help eradicate or better manage your partner's PTSD symptoms. If you are in a new relationship with someone with PTSD, you may be discovering difficulties that you have never faced before. For example, while you always considered yourself a good communicator or problem solver, you seem to be getting nowhere with your new partner. Now, perhaps you can better understand why.

PTSD brings many painful realities. Some may be managed through better communication, negotiation, and problem-solving skills. Then again, some of these skills may seem to make little difference at all in the nature or quality of your relationship. You need to be prepared for this. It does not mean that you are not doing a good job of using these skills. Your loved one may not be able to partner with you to execute them in the ways that are needed. However, with treatment, things may change for both your partner and your relationship. Meanwhile, you may have to use these skills on your own to manage all that you face.

Of course, you may prefer that things were different. But the good news is that you have the ability to do what needs to be done. After all, you have gained new skills and have tapped into the most creative and powerful part of yourself. Don't you feel more personally powerful than you did when you first started reading this book? This is the good that has come from stepping up to the plate and doing what your changed circumstances and relationship have demanded of you. And truly, haven't you discovered that it feels good to grow as a person?

Chapter 10

Coping with Painful Realities

184 Financial Matters

196 Suicide

208 Explosive Anger

When you have a partner with PTSD, things can happen that you'd prefer not to think about—although you truly should. By being prepared for the worst while expecting the best, you may avert painfully challenging times or even a terrible tragedy. For example, your income may suddenly drop if your partner with PTSD can no longer work. Are you prepared to cut household expenses and do you know where to turn for help? As if the financial challenges are not enough, you may face other problems as well. For instance, we know that some people with PTSD will commit suicide. Others will become verbally abusive or even violent despite never previously engaging in such behavior. The question is: If one day your loved one stood there with a gun in hand and made threats against you, himself, or others, would you freeze or remember to call 911? If you have thought about such things ahead of time, you're more likely to take the right action in a crisis situation.

Financial Matters

Has your household income dropped because your partner with PTSD is no longer able to work at the level that he did before? Many couples fight over financial matters anyway, but things could become tense for you in this area if you don't start planning to cut your expenses and begin living on a budget, if your family is not already doing so. Yes, this means forgoing things that you'd all prefer not to give up, but that doesn't mean you can't survive—or even have a good life. You may even find pleasure in coming up with creative ways to confront this challenge. For instance, you could pretend that your family is on a reality television show and, in order to win, you must cut more costs than anyone else—without making the family miserable. By the way, if you come up with some great ideas, feel free to share them at *www.PTSD Relationship.com*.

Budgeting

Before you start to develop a family budget, it may be helpful to do some research. For example, you may get better ideas as to what your family is currently spending not only by looking at your checkbook and old credit card statements, but by having everyone in your household who spends money independently track all the purchases that they make in one month—no matter how small the amount. After all, even small purchases can add up, and they are often the type of expenses that can be cut—such as the cup of coffee purchased on the way to work that could easily be made at home. Everyone could simply list their expenditures in a small pocket notebook.

Once you are ready to start developing a family budget, bring all family members together to participate. Many parents want to hide financial problems from their children, but it's important to discuss how income is spent as a family. Your family also needs you to emphasize what is important, and what is not. Talk about what the family must have in the next week, month, several months, and year. This way, your children will understand why you may need to scale back on purchases and recreational activities. While you don't want to burden children with unnecessary worry, do involve them. They may be able to come up with solutions or ideas that you may not have considered.

With the entire family, first identify what you all absolutely must pay for to survive. Then, start adding in things that you'd all like to have to be more comfortable. After you develop the list together, prioritize the items. You may all need to practice some of the communication, negotiation, and problem-solving skills you learned earlier to accomplish this. Items the family deems of lower priority should be cut first.

Once you have a budget in place, you need to have a means to implement it. There are various ways to do this, but some people like to use an envelope or a jar system that involves cash only. While this is certainly less secure than other methods, this is also the easiest to implement.

Label an envelope or jar for each of the budget categories you establish. You will probably have at least the following:

- Housing and Utilities
- Transportation
- Food
- Medical Care
- Clothing and Personal Care Items
- Entertainment and Recreation
- Savings, Short-term
- Savings, Long-term

Place a predetermined amount or percentage of the weekly, bimonthly, or monthly income into each of the envelopes or jars. The family should not spend more than the amount allocated for each category in the designated time-frame. If there is some type of unexpected expense that comes up in one area—maybe utilities were higher than anticipated because the price of heating oil suddenly increased—the amount should be covered or made up from another category, such as Entertainment and Recreation, that has more flexibility. Then again, you may need to dip into your short-term savings. But do these things first and avoid turning to your credit cards if at all possible.

Other people prefer to use a receipt/account book method. If your family decides to do this, all of your family members should collect receipts for their purchases. These should then be placed in a designated container. At the end of the month, all receipted amounts are placed on a ledger or entered into the computer using a program such as Quicken, so that the spending to date in all categories can be viewed instantly. Of course, with this method, it is easy to mistakenly overspend in certain categories. There may have to be cutbacks made the next month to correct for any over expenditure in one or more areas.

You may also select a checkbook method where you will undoubtedly be the one responsible for paying the bills as well as for doling out predetermined amounts for others to budget and spend.

If you find that you can't pay off all your bills during the course of the month, you'll need to decide which ones to pay first. To do this, you need to set priorities. For instance, you first want to make payments on any secured loans such as your mortgage or your car loan since you don't want to lose either of these. Next, you must pay bills that are for vital services such as utility bills, transportation to get to work, and all necessary insurance policies. Then, look at those expenses that will be the most costly to delay. For example, you'll probably want to pay off credit card bills with the highest interest rate or the worst late-payment penalties before paying off the others.

Since you may struggle to live within the budget you know you now must, let's look at some ways your family might keep costs in check, if not actually decrease them.

Cut Costs

Your family should learn to live on cash to avoid living beyond its means. Furthermore, today you must be careful regarding how you use your credit cards, since many companies are unexpectedly increasing minimum payments, decreasing credit limits, and raising interest rates on cardholders. You could face bills you never expected that turn out to be mostly interest charges and fees.

Everyone in your family should avoid impulse buying by making a shopping list. Also, before you buy anything, ask yourself, *Is this purchase absolutely necessary, or can we live without it for now?* Of course, if you and your family stay out of the stores, you will be less tempted to buy. In addition, stop reading ads and flyers, other than those for your local supermarkets.

You'll want to read the supermarket flyers because it saves money to plan meals around meats, fish, and cheeses on sale. Then, after you've bought these food items, consider fixing dishes and freezing them for the rest of the week's meals so you aren't inclined to buy unhealthy and rather expensive fast food because you don't have something prepared for dinner that night.

Cut down on the use of relatively expensive but easy-to-fix meals by sitting down to dinner as a family at the table. Even if your partner won't join you, feed him whatever the rest of you are eating on a tray in another room, and then try to sit down and dine with the children so you can hear about their day. After all, your children are likely to feel neglected if you don't ensure this special time together. Their PTSD-impacted parent is likely either indifferent or abusive toward them because of avoidance or hyperarousal symptoms. Furthermore, you may be paying scant attention to your children at other times of the day because you're too busy attending to your loved one's needs and all the other demands that PTSD has delivered to your household.

Family members should break the bad habit of eating unhealthy foods between meals—though you may want to keep things like yogurt and fresh fruit on hand for snacks after school. These items aren't inexpensive, but they are no more expensive than the unhealthy snacks, and the children will be getting some of their daily nutrition.

When you must buy something of significant cost, make sure you comparison shop, examine the specials, go to price-competitive stores, ask what the best price is that they can offer you on the item, ask about the possibility of a cash discount, and use coupons if possible. Also, only buy needed clothing and household furnishings, and only when they are on sale unless you're shopping in a store offering sizable discounts already.

If you're shopping the end-of-season clothing sales at a department store, realize that sometimes more-expensive departments mark things down even more than the less-expensive departments, providing great clothes at great prices. So check these out. However, consider the cost of maintaining the garment as well as its cost per wearing. More-costly items probably need to be dry cleaned, but you might be able to use special dry cleaning sheets in the dryer. As far as the cost per wearing of a garment, divide the number of times you assume you will be wearing a garment into the item's cost. You can justify spending more for something that will be worn to work or school regularly versus a dress or shoes for a special party that will likely only be worn once or twice.

Your family can also cut costs by doing the following:

- Repair things rather than replace them if it's economical to do so. Try to eliminate waste.
- Team up with a relative, friend, or neighbor so you can buy in bulk and save that way. Also, borrow each other's tools and equipment rather than buying all your own. Consider trading skills and services with others rather than purchasing all the services you need.
- Postpone the purchases of noncritical items or any remodeling projects until your partner is able to start working again—assuming this is possible, of course.
- Eat out only for special occasions, which means packing a lunch for work. Use the time you no longer spend getting to and from restaurants to walk with a colleague. This is a stress buster, and when you bust stress, you may be less apt to engage in retail therapy.
- Run errands only one or two set days a week. Tell family members if they don't plan ahead, they'll have to do without. Stick to this, and people will learn to plan ahead—although your partner with PTSD might have trouble remembering. Make concessions for her, but train the kids.
- Keep your house warmer in the summer than you've likely been doing, as well as cooler in the winter. Dress in layers so you can either take clothes off or put them on. And realize ceiling fans can be helpful for any season—just reverse the direction in the winter to redistribute the heat that has risen to the ceiling.
- Carpool to work and to get the kids to school and to their after-school activities. Consider divesting yourself of one or more cars after you arrange to carpool, first getting rid of any luxury car that is expensive to maintain. If you're embarrassed that you can't afford these

vehicles, talk about striving to live a greener life and reducing your carbon footprint.

- Go to the local library to read magazines rather than buying them regularly. Also, find out if there are movies you can borrow from the library in lieu of either renting or buying them, unless you're purchasing a title that the children will watch time and again.

- If you've been hiring people to clean the house, mow the lawn, or shovel snow, think about whether you and your children could take these chores on yourselves. If you're self-employed and are, in fact, losing billable hours doing these things when you could be making more money if you turned those chores over to others who charge less than your time is worth, cut expenses elsewhere so you can pay these people until you start generating more income from your work.

- If you smoke, take steps to quit. Go to the American Cancer Society (ACS) website at *www.cancer.org*, and at the column to the left, click on the link for Guide to Quitting Smoking.

- Stop buying season tickets and health club memberships that you aren't really using. Recognize that there might be a cheaper way to get your exercise, such as by walking with your partner instead of going to a club.

- Consider the possibility of refinancing your mortgage if you could save yourself a couple of percentage points. Some homes have gone down in value so much that people can't afford to do this, but check with a reputable bank or lender to see if this is an option for your household.

- Try to cut your income taxes by taking better advantage of itemized deductions. Talk to the Small Business

Administration about either you or your partner establishing a business at home, or make an appointment with your accountant. This would allow for a home office deduction as well as others that are work related.

- If you suspect you're paying more property taxes than you need to, you can appeal your home assessment. Call the assessor's office first to make sure you understand the formula for determining your home's value. Realize that you may have to pay some fees for a reassessment.

- Brainstorm with your partner or with your children to come up with ways to have fun without spending money. You might make a pizza and enjoy a movie from the library together at home, go on a picnic, take advantage of free and low-cost community events, have potluck dinners with friends and family, spend an evening at the library to look at magazines, join a book club, play tennis or other sports at the park, quilt, or go on a nature walk.

Also, if you suspect that your partner's PTSD is going to impact your financial situation for an extended period of time, think about cutting your housing costs by moving to a smaller home or less expensive apartment—perhaps even in a less expensive town or part of the country. Realize that even if you must sell your home at a lower price than you would prefer, this may still prove to be a good move if you can make the numbers work and buy low elsewhere. Of course, you need to consider more than the cost of the house. Be aware of your total tax burden—state income taxes, sales taxes, and property taxes. Know what type of utility costs to expect. Pay attention to what type of commute you may have to work and the costs involved there.

If you suspect that your partner will be dealing with ongoing PTSD problems, you need to research the availability and costs of health care in areas you're considering for relocation. If you have children in school, you should also be concerned about the quality of the schools. There is a lot to think about, but it may well be worth the consideration.

If moving doesn't make sense, think of other ways to decrease the significant cost of home ownership. Could you rent out a room to another? Could you rent out your house and still cover your expenses, and then you and the family live somewhere else for less than you are now? You may want to talk with a real estate agent and your accountant to figure out your options.

Insurance

Depending on your circumstances, insurance may seem a significant cost in your household budget—one that you're even contemplating cutting. If so, think this through carefully. Perhaps rather than dropping policies, carefully reevaluate the policies you have. Make sure you don't have duplicate coverage and see if making changes in any existing policy makes sense and will help you cut costs. For example, you may want to have only liability coverage on an older car. Also, see if you can get a better rate by having all your insurance with one company or agency. You may also be able to purchase insurance more cheaply directly from the company you like to deal with by going through the Internet instead of going through an insurance agency.

If someone in the family needs dental or health care and you believe that you can't afford it because you lack insurance or have a very high deductible, ask the professional you're consulting with if he ever works on a sliding fee. Community agencies may charge based on one's ability to pay. If the professional is part of a large medical facility, talk to people in their billing department and see if they can assist you in any way. If your policy has a high deductible, ask if the medical facility ever offers discounts on medical services for underinsured patients. They may also offer a payment plan that has a lower interest rate than your credit card does. Inquire if they'll adjust your bill on your ability to pay. In addition, consider talking to the social worker affiliated with the medical facility. This professional may have suggestions for getting needed care at a reasonable price or finding financial or other assistance—perhaps through community nonprofit organizations.

You should also look into the possibility of getting any needed medications free of charge from the pharmaceutical company. Go to the company's website and check for this information in their section geared toward patients.

If you don't have medical insurance, check out the costs of things like the use of the emergency room and various procedures at different facilities before a family member has anything done—and before anyone has a medical emergency. The cost of going to one emergency room versus another may vary by hundreds of dollars. And when it comes to procedures, some hospitals charge uninsured patients more than insured ones whereas another may give a discount—or reduce the bill if your income falls below a certain level. Also, avoid going to specialists if possible and rely upon your family physician or perhaps even a nurse practitioner for routine care and illnesses. But check their office visit costs first so you don't get an unpleasant surprise. Someone who handles the physician's billing should have this information.

When you do have an insurance claim—medical or otherwise—be prepared to resubmit it more than once as well as battle to get it paid. Make sure that you keep copies of everything and that you also document all interactions you have with anyone at the insurance company. Don't just write down the names of all the people you talk with, but record the dates, the times, and the nature of results of any and all discussions. If you have the specifics and end up getting different answers than what you were previously told by company representatives, go ahead and ask to have the recordings of your calls pulled. Don't be afraid to stand your ground and demand payment for all services to which you're entitled.

You may also want to put your requests for payment in writing and send them via registered mail. If there is much money at stake or time is of the essence, consider hiring an attorney who specializes in such matters. If your partner is a wounded soldier from Afghanistan or Iraq, you can seek free help from Lawyers Serving Warriors. Otherwise, you may want to contact an attorney who takes cases on contingency— where the attorney takes an established percentage of what is ultimately collected on your behalf. Be sure that you fully understand the nature of the contract with the attorney before signing anything.

Finding Help

You hear ads all the time on television regarding organizations that want to help you deal with your debt and other financial issues. Be wary, as many of these can be scams. Furthermore, just because an organization is a nonprofit doesn't mean that it's trustworthy or will serve you well. Instead, contact your local United Way and see which organizations they fund that may be able to help you. Go to *www.liveunited.org* and enter your zip code in the designated box near the top of the page to locate the address of the office nearest you.

You may also want to contact your local Cooperative Extension System office, part of the USDA's Cooperative State Research, Education, and Extension System. Offices are located in every state's land grant university. To find the office nearest you, go to *www.csrees.usda.gov/Extension*. At your state's Cooperative Extension System office you'll find staff who provide useful, practical, and research-based information to families as well as to small business owners and agricultural producers. They also have programs for youth through 4-H. In some parts of the country, Cooperative Extension is also very involved with helping military families.

Hopefully, you now feel that you have some ways to deal with your family's finances. While things may prove challenging at times, with these resources you may never have to face a situation you can't somehow resolve before matters reach a point of crisis.

Suicide

If your partner is thinking about suicide, you may not even realize it—unless you know how to read the signs. Even if you're seeing or hearing these signs, you may be denying what's happening. This shouldn't be too surprising. Many of us were raised to think that people who contemplated or committed suicide were showing personal weakness, being selfish, or being manipulative. Also, the act of suicide itself was often considered both shameful and sinful. It, of course, makes sense that you may want to ignore the fact that your partner is suicidal, but by doing so, you may not be able to stop him from doing this very thing. Would it help you to lay aside your denial if you knew some of the things that you were told about suicide aren't true?

A person can experience a temporarily changed state of mind and believe the unhealthy voice telling him that the pain and misery being experienced in the moment will be everlasting and unendurable. In this temporarily changed state of mind, suicide is the only option the person perceives as a means to end the pain. This person contemplating suicide just wants the seemingly endless pain to end. Suicide is about ending pain, not about ending one's life.

Suicide is especially prevalent in those who are already suffering from PTSD because many of the conditions associated with an increased risk of suicide are often strongly associated with PTSD. Examples include:

- **Terminal illness, significant injury, or death of a relative or friend:** If your partner is suffering PTSD resulting from trauma suffered in war, he may have seen a good friend die or become badly injured. Even if the PTSD did not stem from war, the traumatic event likely involved death to others as well as significant injury to the PTSD sufferer.
- **Broken relationship, separation, or divorce:** Sadly enough, if PTSD is allowed to proceed untreated, it may put such stress on a relationship that the couple may break up or the marriage may end in divorce.
- **Loss of health:** People are more likely to suffer health problems after developing PTSD. This isn't surprising,

as PTSD often stems from a traumatic event that resulted in bodily, emotional, and spiritual wounds. We
now understand that there is a mind-body connection,
which means that the PTSD sufferer should almost be
expected to experience a loss of health.

- **Loss of job, money, and home as well as the personal security, status, and the self-esteem all these
  provide:** People with PTSD often develop problems
  that are so severe that they cannot maintain their existing level of employment. This results in loss of money,
  personal security, status, and the self-esteem that both
  the job and the money provided.

- **Alcohol or drug abuse:** We've talked about how these
  substances can seem to help PTSD sufferers at first,
  providing a means to self-medicate their symptoms.
  But in time, many sufferers become addicted—and
  they then develop more problems as a result of that
  addiction. Also, remember that the abused substance
  may loosen inhibitions so the PTSD-sufferer becomes
  capable of actually taking his own life.

- **Depression:** The PTSD sufferer is apt to experience
  depression alongside PTSD. Depression leads to changes in the brain and overwhelming feelings of helplessness and hopelessness. These can cause the person to
  step onto that downward spiral toward suicide—especially if no action is taken to stop them.

What's Your Attitude?

If your partner becomes suicidal, she's going to require your
assistance to get the help she needs. How do you feel about
this? You may say that of course you want to help your loved

one. Please, stop and think a minute, though. Do you have beliefs lingering from the past that may get in the way of you stepping up there and doing what needs to be done? Really, this is a serious question. While you may want to believe that you'd never have a problem doing this, you could be holding unconscious beliefs that could stop you, or at least make you hesitate. Since you don't want that to happen, face up to them. Don't blame or condemn yourself for holding these beliefs. Just make a conscious decision that, from now on, you're prepared to step forth and help your partner no matter what you may have been told or believed in the past about people who are suicidal.

Remind yourself that you can't expect your partner, sitting there filled with thoughts of suicide, to seek help on her own. She probably doesn't have the mental wherewithal to take this much-needed step.

To know if you may have to intervene in the near future, have a talk about suicide with your loved one. Ask her if she has ever thought about killing herself. If this has been the case, you want to assess how far down the path toward suicide your partner actually is.

It's Okay to Talk about Suicide

As a child, were you told never to mention suicide around someone who was feeling miserable? Were you told that such an individual was more likely to go forth and commit suicide if you mentioned the word in front of her? Do you believe that this is true? If so, you're operating under a false belief. You may actually prevent your loved one from committing suicide if you can talk openly about this subject.

When you have this talk, you need to be open to questioning your partner and hearing her answers. You want to acknowledge what your partner is saying with calmness and acceptance of the fact that your beloved could truly mean what she is saying in the moment because of a current changed frame of mind. Don't respond by saying something like, "I know you'd never do that." After all, she may jump up and do it right then and there, to show you just how serious she is. You also don't want to put your partner down for having such thoughts. Your goals should be to remain calm, keep your partner calm, and discover the full extent or details about her plan—if indeed there is one.

CASE STUDY

Leah and Jerry

Are you wondering how to go about having a conversation with your loved one about suicide? Read this case study about Leah and her PTSD-suffering husband, Jerry, to see how to go about having this difficult discussion.

Leah: *Jerry, your PTSD symptoms have been getting to you, haven't they?*

Leah knew Jerry had spent a restless night—awakened once again by a bad dream about his accident. Of course, she felt tired as well. She rarely slept through one of Jerry's nightmares. He thrashed about too violently.

Jerry (sighing): *I can't keep living this way.*

Leah (struggling to take a few deep breaths): *Jerry, I realize I have no idea what you've been going through, but it does seem you've been having a really rough time of it lately. I was wondering, do you ever think about suicide?*

Jerry's fingers tapped against the wood of the breakfast table. Leah sat uncomfortably in the silence, waiting for her husband's reply. She finally realized it wasn't going to come, perhaps not without some assurance from her that she perceived thinking about suicide as something other than an extreme or unusual behavior. And because she knew from an article that she had recently read that many people did indeed have passing thoughts of suicide, she mentioned this to her husband.

Jerry (shifting his large frame on the oak chair): *Yeah, I guess the thought has crossed my mind once or twice.*

Leah (laying her hand on Jerry's): *What do you think about exactly when the thought of suicide springs into your mind?*

Leah asked this as calmly as possible. She wanted Jerry to sense she was open to hearing whatever he wanted to share with her—she wasn't there to judge him, lay a guilt trip on him, or convince him that suicide was a bad idea—because he had so much to live for instead. Today's discussion was about discovering where Jerry was on what may be called the path to suicide. Had he only had passing thoughts about suicide, or was he further along down that path? Did he have a fully developed plan that he was ready to execute?

Jerry: *I sometimes figure you and the kids would be better off without me. You don't need me going around and exploding at you all the time, do you?*

New thoughts sprang into Leah's mind. Jerry certainly wasn't the man she had fallen in love with and married. That Jerry had been more easygoing, and had always been kind. Now her husband could say the cruelest things. Leah was having trouble dealing with all those hurtful remarks—even though she kept reminding herself that it was the PTSD talking, not the man she had long loved. However, that didn't change the fact that she was bombarded by such negativity on a daily basis. While Jerry had obviously been wondering how much longer he could live this way, the same question had been crossing Leah's mind with greater frequency. The difference was, she wasn't suicidal. She realized that Jerry could be, however, and she needed to deal with that.

Leah (touching her husband's hand): *I've been hoping that the new medication you started last week would kick in and start working.*

Jerry: *I killed two people. That car accident was my own fault. Those people are dead because of me. How can I live with that?*

Leah: *Technically, that's true, but how could you have changed the outcome, Jerry? Your car hit a huge patch of ice. It spun out of control. Why do you keep blaming yourself for something over which you had no control—other than you were out there driving to meet the demands of your job?*

Jerry: *I was in a rush. I was going too fast for the weather conditions. I have to live with that.*

Leah: *Are you saying that the emotional pain is too much?*

Leah tried to push back the anxiety arising within her. She knew she needed to understand how severe Jerry's emotional pain was—how far down the road toward suicide he had been pushed.

Jerry: *I've been saving up the sleeping pills the doctor gave me. I've been thinking that some night after I wake up from yet another one of those nightmares, I just might take them.*

Leah thought about how the doctor had told her he'd intentionally given Jerry something to help him sleep that he couldn't use to commit suicide. However, while she was relieved to realize that Jerry wasn't in imminent danger because of that, it was bad news that he had both thought of suicide and had a plan. Sure, it wasn't a plan that would work, but Jerry was obviously oblivious to that. What was important was that her husband was in an emotional frame of mind that would lead him to come up with a plan in the first place.

Leah: *So, you've really been thinking pretty seriously about this, haven't you?*

Jerry: *Yeah, I guess I have been.*

Leah: *Jerry, I would have felt awful if you had killed yourself without warning. I would have felt like I'd let you down. I'm glad I asked the question.*

Jerry: *I don't feel so overwhelmed right now.*

Leah: *Will you promise me you won't commit suicide without first talking to me and telling me what's going on in your*

*mind? That way, I'll have the chance to get you some imme-
diate help. Can you promise me that?*

Jerry agreed and Leah called his doctor and asked for advice. She wanted to believe that Jerry wouldn't go through with
suicide after pledging to her that he would not. But since he
had arranged a plan and had acted on making it workable, that
told her Jerry had walked far down the path toward suicide.
So she needed someone to help her develop a plan of her
own—to help ensure Jerry remained safe. He needed to have
a chance to benefit from treatment before he decided that life
wasn't worth living.

Warning Signs

A number of people have passing thoughts about killing
themselves. Fortunately for most, that's the extent of things.
But some people think thoughts, say things, and behave in
ways that show that they're giving serious thought to suicide.
In the previous case study, Leah didn't realize—at least until
she asked Jerry flat out—that her husband was giving suicide
serious thought, and he had actually devised a plan. But many
people who ultimately attempt or commit suicide give warning through the type of things they say such as:

- I am a horrible person. I did terrible things to others. I
  don't deserve to live.
- My family would be better off without me.
- It's hopeless. I can never get myself out of this mess.
- Life isn't worth living now that I've lost (my wife, my
  children, my job, my house, my reputation, the in-

nocent self I believed myself to be, or whatever else is causing the person great agony or grief), so I may as well be dead.

- I am worthless. I'm just taking up space and wasting precious resources. I don't do enough to deserve to live.
- Life is so painful and difficult. I can't take any more of this.
- How can I go on living when the person I was before has essentially died? That (war, rapist, murderer, thief, accident, or whatever triggered the traumatic event that resulted in the PTSD) killed my spirit and any chance for happiness. What's the point of going on?
- Things will only get worse. Why keep on living?
- No one cares what happens to me anyway. In their minds, I'm already dead.
- How can I ever live down what I did? I'll never be able to put this behind me.
- Why don't you all just leave me alone? Can't you see I think all the things you're doing are stupid and a waste of my time and energy?
- So what if I got a bad review at work? Nothing in this world matters anymore anyway.
- I feel like killing people. (This person probably feels both homicidal and suicidal. He may well kill himself after killing others, or else expect the police to do something he can't bring himself to do—kill him after he has taken the lives of others).

Okay, so these are the types of thoughts that suggest a person may be suicidal. But what behaviors would your partner engage in that would suggest that he may be suicidal? Your partner may do one or more of the following:

- Engage in reckless behaviors or activities that he didn't before.
- Socially isolate himself, or refuse to do things with others that he previously enjoyed.
- Go around visiting old friends and relatives to say good-bye to them.
- Give away valued personal possessions.
- Show either a new or a renewed interest in guns.
- Seek out sleeping pill prescriptions from multiple physicians or other sources.
- Abuse alcohol and/or drugs more so than previously.
- Take out additional life insurance (although life insurance typically will not pay off in the case of suicide).
- Make mini-attempts at suicide. He will do something that he doesn't expect will result in death, but that others might notice and see as his cry for help. Since he's probably beyond the point of seeking help for himself, he needs someone to intervene. Therefore, he may call someone before taking an overdose of pills or may only lightly cut his wrists.
- Make some of the explicit statements of suicidal ideation or feelings that we've already discussed.
- Develop a suicide plan, acquire whatever is needed to carry it out, rehearse the behavior, and set a date and time to complete the suicide.

If your partner is saying or doing these types of things, you need to have that suicide talk sooner rather than later. Assess how far down the path toward suicide he may be, and then decide how rapid your intervention needs to be as well. Remember, when your partner can tell you not only that he has thought about suicide, but also that he has a plan and has taken the steps to make that plan workable, you may also want to ask him if he has a place and date in mind. If the time is soon and your partner has the means to get to that place, you not only need to take immediate action but probably don't want to leave him alone until help arrives.

In this situation, remove everything you can think of that your partner could use to kill himself with. But also watch your loved one like a hawk. Realize that if he feels desperate, he may do something like break a mirror and then use the ragged edge to slash his wrists. Your loved one may think to do things you probably would never consider, so you need to be there trying to keep him calm and watching closely until the much-needed help arrives.

Where can you find that help? You can always call 911, but you may also want to locate a crisis phone number to call for your area of your state. You can find this information at *http://mentalhealth.samhsa.gov/hotlines/state.asp*. Verify now that the number given for your region of your state is still the correct one. When you know that it is, put it on the list where you keep all your emergency phone numbers.

You can even tell your partner that you're going to put it there. Remember, your loved one is aware that he is behaving differently and is not his normal self. He undoubtedly feels badly about this. But while there is a good chance he is not going to intervene on his own behalf—rather, you're going to have to be the one to do this—there is the chance that the day may come when your loved one realizes that he is out of control and needs to talk to someone. Let your partner know the number is there for when he decides he's ready for that discussion. Frame your statement along the lines of: "In case I'm out of the house some day when you're really feeling badly and like you might do something to yourself or someone else—which we both know PTSD could push you to do—I've placed an emergency number (wherever it is). Go ahead and call them immediately. There will be someone there to talk to you and guide you."

While the people who answer these crisis lines can offer guidance, you may feel better contacting your local mental health agency. Of course, if your partner has already overdosed, for instance, you would call an ambulance to take him to the emergency room of the nearest hospital. Once the immediate emergency is handled, they may recommend that he be transferred to another facility where it is possible for him to receive quality psychiatric care.

Let's spell out something carefully here. If your gut is telling you to take action while another voice is going off in your head telling you that you're making too big a deal out of what's happening, listen to your gut and make that call. Remember, it is always better to be safe than sorry.

Explosive Anger

You do need to be concerned about another potential problem: taking the brunt of your partner's irritation and anger. Be aware that PTSD might drive your partner to become abusive toward you—and your children. While this is something you may not want to think about, you must for your own safety.

Those with PTSD often struggle with irritation, if not intense or explosive anger. This is not pleasant, but hopefully it will remain nothing more than that—something unpleasant for you to cope with until your partner can better manage those PTSD symptoms. However, some people with PTSD will act more like the abusive men you've undoubtedly heard about throughout the years—men that women are often forced to leave because they feel so unsafe in their relationships. While your partner may have been the nicest person before developing PTSD, you can't allow yourself to be seduced into a false sense of security by clinging to the image of the man he was before. You need to be prepared to take action to protect yourself and your children if things are getting out of hand. You also need to realize that, while you're hoping the treatment of the PTSD may return the man you knew previously, you could actually be in danger until then.

Here's an important question: Are there guns in your house? If so, try to get them out of your home if at all possible. Perhaps you don't think that you dare do this because your partner may harm you if he caught you removing them, or once he realized they were gone. Under such circumstances, you may want to talk to your local police about how to best handle the situation. Also, ask about where you might store the weapons in your local area if you don't know of anyone who can safely do this for you.

If you suspect that you're living in the midst of a relationship that could become unsafe at any time, you need to have a safety plan. It will help you take the right actions plus ensure that you have the types of things you need should you have to get out of the house suddenly. A safety plan will also help reduce the risk that either you or the children will be harmed during the process of leaving, or after you have left. After all, while this isn't something you want to think about, you need to realize that violent men are more apt to severely hurt or kill the women in their lives when those women leave, or shortly afterward. Thus, it may be best to try to do what your partner wants in the moment to calm him down. Then, if you feel too unsafe to remain with him, plan to leave when he isn't home.

Furthermore, it may be a good idea to talk to your local police and perhaps involve them when you're leaving.

To help you develop a safety plan, check out the American Bar Association at *www.abanet.org/tips/dvsafety.html* or the National Domestic Violence Hotline at *www.ndvh.org*.

Also, start thinking about your own unique situation and the things that you must plan for as well—such as your children's special needs, pets, or family treasures that you'd hate to leave behind or possibly see destroyed. However, with regard to the latter, you might also want to remind yourself that in the scheme of things, material possessions aren't that significant. The health and well-being of you and your children are paramount.

Here's another thing to think about: What if things get so out of control that you feel forced to flee without your children? Do you dare do that, or will Social Services take them away because of abandonment on your part? If you suspect that this could happen, you may want to talk to the police or Social Services now about how to handle this situation to avoid jeopardizing the future custody of your children. You may also want to seek legal advice. Document what you're told by anyone and everyone. List the people spoken to, the dates, and what they said.

Hopefully, your situation will never get this bad. But again, it is always best to plan for the worst and expect the best.

Chapter 11

Meeting Your Children's Needs

212 Children Are Not Resilient

213 The Aftermath of Vietnam

216 Avoiding a Painful Legacy

231 New Rules and Interactions

211

Are you concerned about how your partner has been treating the children since developing PTSD? Of course, along with everything else, this is going to affect your relationship. So let's look at some of the issues that you may never have thought about—because they weren't issues before PTSD entered your lives. By the way, some of this information may prove relevant even if your partner is a more recent addition to your life, and is not your children's parent. However, it will be most applicable if your children are dealing with a parent recently changed by PTSD.

Children Are Not Resilient

Have you been focusing your full attention on your partner, assuming that your children are resilient and able to deal with whatever life tosses their way? This may seem to be true if you're confusing surviving with thriving. Indeed, children do seem to be capable of surviving all sorts of horrific things simply because they have little choice but to do so. They develop defense mechanisms that help them get through difficult times, but not without repercussions. Furthermore, these defense mechanisms often get in the way once these children enter adulthood, keeping them from developing the desired type of relationship with a romantic partner or attaining closeness with their own children. In fact, rather than risk passing down a hurtful legacy, some will avoid marrying or having children—not because this is what they truly want, but because they feel that they are damaged goods. They believe that if they were to proceed and have families, they may be a cause of harm to their own children.

You don't want your children to grow up into wounded adults. You stand a better chance of avoiding this if you realize and admit that children are not resilient, but rather they are survivors. You want to set your children up to thrive in life, not merely survive.

The Aftermath of Vietnam

You may know that many children of Vietnam War veterans were impacted by growing up with fathers who had lost their capability to form intimate connections with their children and their wives. These soldiers who were wounded by PTSD—although, remember, society did not know what PTSD was at the time—often wanted to be left alone. Certainly, their children craved their love—because it is normal and healthy to both want to receive as well as to give love—and wanted the attention of these men who were emotionally crippled by PTSD. Unfortunately, rather than having this need met, these children often faced fathers who spewed forth anger due to PTSD's hyperarousal symptom.

These children felt painfully rejected, but didn't understand what was happening. Like many children who face such painful things, they often blamed themselves for the problem. They believed that what happened had occurred because they were bad, which caused these children to come to harbor feelings of not being good enough. In fact, such children may have come to feel worthless and carried that feeling with them as they grew into adulthood. Fortunately, with the information that you're learning, your children don't have to suffer this type of experience.

---------------   CASE STUDY   ---------------

Patti and Rachael

Both sisters, Patti and Rachael, sensed from an early age that there was something wrong with their father—that this Vietnam War veteran was wounded in some way emotionally. They both believed that he needed their help and support while, in turn, they sought his love. But this man, for seemingly no reason at all from their perspective, would often suddenly transform into a scary figure.

"There was this way his eyes changed. I knew at that point he was no longer in control of his body," Patti, the younger sister, reported of her early childhood experiences. But this did not stop her from sometimes fighting back verbally at the cruel things her father might say. "I knew you weren't sup-posed to talk the way he did—that the things he said were wrong because they were mean." But of course, talking back only made matters worse. Her father would attack back—likely driven by the PTSD our society had not yet identified, and hence could not treat. Furthermore, in this particular case the veteran was probably set up to develop PTSD because he'd been emotionally wounded by his father, an angry man who may have developed PTSD while serving in the military during World War II.

At times, both girls hid out, Patti sometimes in her bedroom closet. She reported how she had drilled a hole in the wall so she could remain within the closet's confines—which felt safer to her than merely being in her room—but at the same time she could observe her father walking the hall, giving her the opportunity to detect his likely current mood.

Rachael, the older sister who hadn't made such a peep-hole, was more inclined to disappear. "I made myself scarce so as not to become the target of my father's anger. But at the same time, I felt anger toward my mother for not putting her foot down—for not refusing to accept my father's behavior or protecting us from it." She quickly added, "Of course, I realize now she didn't have the knowledge and tools to take such action."

Their mother had grown up in an era and social climate where women were expected to stand by their men and keep their families together at all costs. While it is difficult enough to be a single mother today, it was much more difficult then.

And while the mother sought out the advice of therapists, some of what these therapists—who didn't know or understand anything at all about PTSD—encouraged her to do only made matters worse. These therapists did not understand how this disorder may play out in the family—and impact the children in particular.

Both Patti and Rachael were left with emotional scars from having grown up with a war veteran father with untreated PTSD. Both had accepted responsibility for the problem of their father's anger and abusive behavior. Both became wrapped in feelings of not being good enough because of this personal history. Patti and Rachael also both went on to have problems in adulthood creating the type of lives that they'd once imagined for themselves, likely because they'd endured this painful legacy.

Avoiding a Painful Legacy

The sisters in the case study sensed that there was something wrong with their father, but were never told that their father had an illness. Of course, no one knew what PTSD was, but it may have helped if their mother had admitted that their father seemed to be having emotional problems that had nothing to do with them—that he had been changed by war. Instead, these daughters of a PTSD-suffering war veteran felt they were treated as if they had not been perceiving things correctly. One even felt that she was made out to be a liar.

By essentially having the realities they experienced during their childhood negated by their mother, Patti and Rachael grew into women who took their father's anger—and the hurtful things he'd said about them—to heart. It wasn't until they were much older that they realized their father's lack of affection stemmed from his mental health issue of PTSD, not from their bad behavior or the fact they were unlovable human beings.

Patti and Rachael's mother wishes that she had had the knowledge of PTSD back then that she has today as a clinical social worker. She is certain she would have handled things differently.

Indeed, since we now know about PTSD, you *can* handle things differently. Your children will be helped by the fact that you can be open and talk about the PTSD that is impacting your family system. Hopefully, as a result, your children will enter adulthood realizing that they faced some painful consequences of their father's PTSD, but that how they were treated was not their fault and spoke nothing of their worth as people. It only spoke of their parent's mental disorder.

Of course, it may be hard for you to accept that your part-ner has changed and, as a result, may be incapable of express-ing love—until he receives treatment for PTSD, that is. How-ever, while this can be upsetting for you to face, remember that it is more upsetting for your children. While you can remind yourself that the PTSD is talking when your partner does or says hurtful things, your children probably will not understand why a parent who loved them—and was able to express that love before—has seemed to have turned on them. And again, this is how they are apt to perceive things, that the parent turned on them because they were bad or worthless.

Please realize that your children are going to be distressed at the apparent loss of the parent's love. They may even fight back with angry words of their own. For example, a child whose father has combat-related PTSD may say something like "You are not my Daddy. Go back to the war. I don't want you here anymore." Needless to say, because the parent with PTSD has an impaired brain, he is not apt to react like a ratio-nal adult. Instead, the parent will likely lash back defensively, causing matters to worsen.

Talk Freely

You need to explain in simple terms, or in terms appro-priate to the ages of your children, that their parent is sick. You may point out that—as when they are sick with a cold or stomachache—their mother is irritable and will lash out in anger. And while their parent would not have said mean or hurtful things before, she is apt to say them now purely be-cause of the illness. You may then talk to your children about putting up an imaginary shield or stepping into a protective bubble, which will keep the parent's hurtful words away—and from wounding the child's heart, spirit, or soul.

――――――――――― CASE STUDY ―――――――――――

Mother and Child

Let's take a look at how a mother's conversation with her child about his father's PTSD may unfold.

Mother: *Remember the time you felt really bad because you had a tummy ache? You didn't want to talk to other people, did you? And didn't you feel like you could get angry easily, too?*

Child: *I guess so.*

Mother: *Well, Daddy isn't well right now, either. Being over there in that war made him sick. The thing is, he will be sick much longer than you were with your tummy ache.*

Child: *But he doesn't have to stay in bed.*

Mother: *No, his sickness is a little different. He can be up and around. However, his sickness makes him not want to do things with us. He also doesn't like to talk to us.*

Child: *He talks. He says mean things to me.*

Mother: *I know that happens. He gets angry and mean because of his sickness. I don't think he would ever say or do those things if he wasn't sick.*

Child: *He would still love me like he did before—instead of hating me?*

Mother (giving child a hug): *Oh, no, your Daddy doesn't hate you. His sickness makes him do things that seem that way, though. Even though he doesn't hate you, those things he does still really hurt, don't they? If we can help Daddy get better, he should stop being so mean.*

Child: *How can I help him get better?*

Mother: *Well, it might help Daddy if you could save your noisy play for outside or in your room—and try to do something quiet like look at a book when you are in the same room with your Dad. Do you think you could do that?*

Child (pouting): *I want him to play with me like he did before.*

Mother: *I know. I want your Daddy to go on trips to Grandma's and to do other things he doesn't want to do now. It makes me feel sad, too, that he wants to stay home alone.* **(Pauses)** *Anyway, it is okay to be sad about how Daddy acts now that he is sick.*

Child: *Will he get better if I'm quiet?*

Mother: *It may not make him all better, but it will probably help him feel better—just like when you and I are sick, we like quiet, right?*

Child: *I guess so.*

Mother: *You should come to Mommy and tell me if you are feeling sad or hurt because of the things that Daddy does or says. Try to do this instead of yelling at him and telling him not to do that, okay?*

Child: *But he does things that aren't nice.*

Mother: *I know that, and I am sorry he hurts you because of his sickness. But I need to hear about those things so I can talk to him in a special way that he can hear—without getting mad.*

Child: *Like me using my soft voice instead of my angry voice?*

Mother: *Yes, something like that. I can say things to him that he will listen to because I am his wife. He gets angry when you say those things because you are his child.*

Child: *He hurts my feelings!*

Mother: *I understand, and I can see why you feel that way. The next time that happens, can you tell yourself in your head that Daddy's sickness is spewing forth those words like a dragon might spew forth fire? And then, come and tell me what he said and how it made you feel. We can talk about it until you feel better. Will that work?*

Child: *Will that help Daddy get better faster?*

Mother: *I think it just might.*

If you have older children, you may want to talk with them about some of the defense mechanisms they may currently be using to survive in your stressful and likely chaotic home environment. For example, maybe your preteen has learned to keep her mouth shut at home—to not ask questions or express opinions that could trigger the PTSD-impacted parent's anger. But if she has carried this into the classroom at school, could it be harming her performance or grades? Is she avoiding being the type of active participant that the teacher desires and that may facilitate the educational process? If you suspect that this may be the case, talk to your child about defense mechanisms and how, while they may help her survive the painful home environment, they could sabotage her in the real world.

Help your child to formulate ways to continue to behave at home as necessary, but to then have the flexibility in behavior to act differently in other environments. Of course, this is a great skill for anyone to have. You may help your child realize that by developing this ability, she will have gained something positive from having lived with a parent with PTSD. However, while you want to help your child see that negative life events can present opportunity as well as emotional pain, you don't want to dismiss what she is going through. Allow her to vent her feelings to you. Provide an opening for your child to talk about her struggles whenever the need arises.

Despite the fact that you want to be there for your children, you may realize that things aren't going well. They aren't talking to you. They may be acting out. You need to accept that, as much as you want to help them, they may need someone else to listen to them—perhaps a therapist. You may all meet with the therapist together in family therapy, or the therapist may recommend individual therapy for one or more of the children instead.

Dysfunctional Roles of Dysfunctional Families

We have learned from studying families with an alcoholic parent that children often assume unhealthy roles to help them deal with the stresses that come with dysfunctional family life. While different people may label some of these roles differently, you may observe your child becoming:

- The family hero
- The family mascot or clown
- The scapegoat
- The caregiver or surrogate parent
- The surrogate spouse
- The lost child

To help you see if this emotionally unhealthy scenario is playing out in your family—or to alert you that it could— let's talk about each of these roles briefly.

The Family Hero

The family hero tries not only to do everything right, but to be the best at anything taken on. This is the child who becomes the high achiever or outstanding performer. Now, while it may seem a good thing that a child goes forth and does outstandingly well, it actually isn't in a dysfunctional family.

The child may feel driven to do these things not because they make his heart sing or are a fit with his interests or natural talents, but from emotional reasons. Often, at an unconscious level, the child is striving to do well to gain the approval of the likely critical and disapproving parent. The child may also want to distract others from looking too closely at what is really going on in the household. He may be thinking something along the lines of: If I look and act perfect, others may assume things are perfect in my home, too. I won't have to deal with the shame of them discovering the truth. I can keep the family secret hidden—something my parents want as well.

If you have a child playing this role, it may be easy to breathe a sigh of relief, essentially ignore him, and be glad that you can dedicate yourself more fully to the needs of your partner. Don't do this. Instead, realize that your child undoubtedly needs your support.

Talk to your child about his successes. Don't minimize them or, in fact, your child may struggle to do even better yet. Rather, talk to him about how life demands balance. Are there other things this child would prefer to be doing or that he would like to try? Don't assume your child has found nirvana. He may be approaching life in a way that will lead to burnout, not the sustained success you may hope for him.

The Family Mascot or Clown

Have you ever heard a comedian talk about his childhood? Many will indicate that they faced emotionally painful challenges in their early years. They dealt with these issues by becoming the funny kid—making jokes about human behavior rather than being brought down by the pain.

In many dysfunctional families, a child will either become the cute one that everyone adores—taking on the family mascot role—or by becoming the family clown. Both are a means of distracting the self—and others—from the painful realities of what is going on. And while there is the chance that the child may become a successful stand-up comedian or talk-show host from having this well-developed skill, the odds are that this will not happen. She may make everyone else laugh while she is crying inside.

Don't merely be grateful that you have a child who can break up the tension in your household by making you all laugh. Yes, laughter is important, but look behind the jokes. Make certain that you're not laughing at everything this child says or does without looking at what may be going on for your child emotionally. You may want to say something every once in a while to this child such as, "We all enjoy your jokes, and they ease some of the emotional pain that we all feel. But we not only need to laugh, but to have some serious talks regarding how we feel about what is happening because of PTSD's presence in our lives. So, can we talk about how things are for you right now—and leave the jokes out of it for the time being?"

The Scapegoat

There is often a child in the family who becomes the scapegoat. Rather than be honest about the problems the family faces and confront them at the source—by, for instance, ensuring that your partner's PTSD symptoms are dealt with—you may blame your child for the family's problems instead. How does this occur?

Often, a child will become upset at what is going on and begin to act out as a result of personal emotional pain. Rather than admitting that all of this may stem from the fact that the child must cope with so many painful changes as a result of that unwelcome guest, PTSD, one or both parents may label the child as the problem; after all, for them, this may be easier than dealing with how the PTSD has put their relationship—among other things—on a downward trajectory. The child may then become confused because what he perceives as happening is being denied. For example, the child may be abused by the parent with PTSD, while others tell him that this isn't happening. The child then gets the message that the parent sees him as either a liar or as someone who is crazy and out of touch with reality. Either outcome is painful.

This is a very damaging role for a child to have to play. So, if one of your youngsters begins to act out, get him professional help if necessary. But please, do not label your child as the problem. Instead, view your child's behavior as a barometer of what is going on in your home. Realize that your child is simply reacting to the home environment that you and your partner have created. Because of the PTSD, it may be impossible for you to create the type of home life that you'd prefer for your children. This is sad, but it is also the truth. The thing is, this truth will be less damaging to your children if you share it with them—and if you hear how this truth is impacting them as well.

Sometimes children need little more than to feel that they have been heard. When a child is acting out, remind yourself this might be the issue—your child feels her cries are landing on deaf ears. Open yours, however, and things may change. Your child may not feel the need to act out any longer. Remember, this behavior drew attention—and to a child, even negative attention is better than no attention at all.

The Caregiver or Surrogate Parent

While parents are assigned the caregiver roles in the family, sometimes—because of an illness such as PTSD—a parent is unable to fulfill this role and its duties. When this happens, a child may step in and take on this burden. The child may do this because she is essentially forced into taking on the role by one or both parents—or because she realizes that if she doesn't do this, all members of the family are going to suffer. For example, none of the children in the family may get fed or have clean clothes, if this child—likely the oldest girl—doesn't take on the role.

While a child should be asked to help out and take on one or more assigned household tasks that are age appropriate, a child should never have to become a caregiver. If one of your children is playing the caregiver role now, admit this to yourself. Then decide to do something to change things.

To find ways to assign duties and get some of the help that you need while you remain in the driver's seat, check out the University Cooperative Extension at *http://extension.unh.edu/ family/documents/Chores.htm*. But again, remember that as the parent, it is your responsibility to remain the caregiver, no matter what is going on in your own life.

The Surrogate Spouse

Sometimes a child will fall into playing the role of a surrogate spouse, which means that the child is treated as if he is the partner—usually because the PTSD partner can no longer meet his spouse's emotional needs. Now, while a child may be sexually abused in this situation, this isn't typically the case. Rather, the child is often leaned upon emotionally or used as a confidant. The parent who is struggling with the needs of her PTSD partner and the household may share these struggles with the child. This parent may expect the child to be there and do things with her because her partner no longer provides such companionship.

Please do not put your child in this position. Your intentions may be innocent enough, but the consequences are not. Many children who have had to play this role end up with some of the problems that can be seen in those who were actually sexually abused. It can result in something some have referred to as emotional incest. Remember, your child is not equipped to play this role. He is not your best friend—even if the child is a teenager. Let your children be children. Confide in a close friend or family member. Go to a support group. Find yourself a therapist. But do not force one of your children into this emotionally dangerous role.

The Lost Child

With all the challenges your partner with PTSD brings, it may be a relief to have a lost child. After all, this is the child who strives to disappear into the woodwork—to become scarce or invisible. This child may hang out alone in her room. However, she may also become quite depressed and lonely, and may harbor bad feelings about herself. Also, if your child hangs out online on social networking sites or chat rooms, she may become easy prey for a pedophile looking for a child whose parents are distracted because of illness or other reasons. Your child needs to know that she is safe because you are there to fulfill your roles as both a parent and an adult. Don't let your child become lost, but instead, structure times for interaction.

Assuring Your Children

Make sure your children know that you are there for them. This includes protecting them from the potential abusiveness their PTSD-impacted parent may impart. Keep giving your children the message that you want to know if their parent with PTSD hurts them in any way. Remember, your children may not feel comfortable coming to you if you only relay this message once or twice. It is important that it be repeated, so that, hopefully, if something does happen, the child has heard the message recently enough to feel comfortable coming forward and talking with you.

To be there for your children, you may have to behave in ways that go against the type of parent you'd prefer to be. For example you may not be able to have the type of open communication about your children and their problematic behaviors that you'd prefer to have with your partner. Whereas normally it is suggested that a couple parent together and present a united front, you may have to keep things from your partner if he is apt to overreact and become abusive, either physically or verbally.

You may have to hear and accept as possibilities things about your partner that may be painful to acknowledge. But to support and be there for your children, you need to do this. Again, keep stressing to your children that they can come to you and express their concerns and fears. Then make sure you walk the walk. If you hear things that you'd prefer not to believe, tell yourself that under these circumstances, your children have little reason to lie. Remember, the odds are that the children want the love of that parent. So, when any child reports something that is the antithesis of loving behavior, that child is likely hurting emotionally. Furthermore, a child cannot intervene against a parent on his own behalf. It is your role as the adult, the parent, and the partner of the PTSD sufferer to step up to the plate and assume responsibility for what is happening—and take actions to protect your children.

Setting Boundaries

What do you do if one or more of your children are being hurt by your PTSD-impacted partner? Well, you will need to talk to your partner and set some boundaries. Make sure your partner understands that certain behaviors are off limits as far as the children are concerned. Help your partner realize that he will be held accountable for harmful behavior despite the presence of PTSD.

You may not want to tell your partner that the child came and complained to you because this could set the child up for further attack. What could you tell your partner instead? You many want to mention that you've noticed how he seems to be having more trouble being around the children in recent days. Then, you may want to ask your partner what any or all of you can do to give him the necessary space to heal—while ensuring that the children's well-being is not put at risk while this is taking place. See what ideas your partner has. If they seem reasonable, and you agree they could be good interventions, agree that you'll try them with the children.

Of course, your partner may not have suggestions. He may also not see where any of his behavior toward the kids has been inappropriate. In this case, you may have to be even clearer about setting these boundaries. Tell your partner that you can't let specific behaviors take place—and spell them out. You may want to further explain that, because you aren't always going to be there to see everything, you are going to encourage the children to report anything that happens that they know is wrong. Also, you are always going to look into such matters because, while you love her and want to be supportive, your first priority must be the safety and well-being of your children. After all, they are children. There is no one else to act as their advocate. As an adult with PTSD, your partner has numerous professionals to whom he may turn.

The Primary Disciplinarian

You probably feel overwhelmed already, so you may not like to hear that you may well need to become your children's primary disciplinarian. This is, in part, because your partner may want to retreat from family life and take on no responsibility for the children. Since children don't do well at raising themselves, however, you're going to have to step forward and take on this task. You may also need to become the disciplinarian because your partner may not have adequate self-control to perform this role safely at this point in time. After all, she is likely to become irritated or angry. If you allow your partner to become the disciplinarian, she may become too harsh, even abusive, with the children. You obviously don't want that to happen.

This book is not about discipline techniques, so we won't go into them in any detail here. But please do understand that while you may or may not agree, hitting or spanking a child shouldn't be in any parent's discipline toolbox. Also, realize that while using time-outs can be a good tactic for young children who are being aggressive and acting out of control, it is sometimes overused by parents and preschool teachers, or applied to too many behaviors that parents wish to extinguish. Used improperly, time-out can have a detrimental effect on a child's emotional well-being. Furthermore, it may not keep the child from engaging in the undesired behaviors again. A better approach for handling less problematic behaviors is to walk over to the child, state what the child is doing wrong, and provide a more appropriate alternative. So, if your child is jumping on the couch, you may say, "Couches are for sitting, not jumping upon. Why don't you go get a book—and then you can sit on the couch and look at it."

Because of the unique circumstances that you find yourself in, you may have to discipline a child for misbehavior and leave it at that. Don't plan to tell your partner about the child's actions if you know this is likely to make her angry—thus setting the child up for abuse. When a situation like this arises with a slightly older child who can understand, you could say something like, "I'm not going to tell your Mom about this because we both know that this would probably get her upset, which will only make her PTSD symptoms worse. I'm going to assume that you understand that this was the wrong thing to do, and you're not going to do it again. Can I count on you? Do you know what you should do if you ever face this type of situation again?"

If the child doesn't know a more appropriate alternative behavior, then discuss potential solutions. Otherwise, trust that your child understands that, just because you are not going to tell the other parent, this does not mean that he is essentially off the hook and can act this way again. Hopefully, the child will realize that you are trying to protect him from the likely irrationality of the parent with PTSD—and will appreciate this enough to try to adhere to your wishes henceforth.

New Rules and Interactions

Because of the way PTSD has changed things, it may be time to realize that the old rules your family abided by no longer serve you. If you never had any rules, it may be important to take the time to establish some. One way you can do this—as well as delegate family tasks—is to hold a weekly family meeting. (And by the way, all children should be able to participate as long as they know how to talk.) Again, while a family meeting should involve everyone, you may discover that your partner is unwilling or unable to participate. If this is the case, you should go ahead and have these meetings alone with your children. After your partner has been in treatment for the PTSD for a while, you may try again to get him involved.

Family Meetings

What follows are some specifics about the family meeting. There may be a reference made to your partner being there. If he will not be for one reason or another, proceed to do on your own what both parents were designated to do. That said, here are some guidelines to follow.

First, have everyone in the family come together and arrange a weekly meeting time and place. No one should have to give up a favorite previously scheduled activity in order to attend these meetings—the time and place should work for everyone week after week. If someone's schedule changes because of work or such, you may need to change the time of the meeting every once in a while. However, don't let the kids get the idea this isn't important because you agree to shift the time.

As the parents, you should serve as co-moderators for the first few meetings. Then, after several weeks, share this role with the children so everyone is familiar with how these sessions should proceed. During the first meeting, you should all decide together how these meetings will operate and then plan to adhere to the rules that you have established. Write them out on a piece of poster board and always bring this to the meetings. If anyone gets out of line, rather than attacking the person, point to the rule being violated. These procedures and rules should allow everyone to contribute to the conversation equally, ensure that each person is listened to fully by the others, and promote supportive behavior. Even when family members disagree, it's important that you all still support each other's willingness to be an active member of the process—for giving other family members food for thought.

Throughout the course of the meeting, the moderator should ensure that all family members have a chance to speak on each and every topic raised. Whoever is filling this role should keep going around the circle asking each person to give input on the current topic. No one should make a comment on what another may say, other than to ask questions to clarify what the person meant. Do not allow people to argue or make the speaker wrong.

Each meeting should begin with every family member talking about something that happened—inside or outside the family—that made him feel good that week. As the parents, you and your partner should offer praise, encouragement, and support for the good thing each child mentions. If your partner is incapable of doing this, take on this task yourself—and make sure your partner doesn't become critical during this exercise.

Next, each person should point out something that bothered him that week. As the parents, you and your partner should listen for and acknowledge the feelings lying behind the incident divulged. Since your partner might not be able to do this as a healthy adult would, plan to do it yourself. It may be necessary to say something to the child such as: "When that happened, it sounds like you felt both sad and scared." You would then check back with the child and say, "Is that how you felt, or did you feel something else instead?"

If a child brings up a problem that the entire family has some control over and could fix, you might ask: "What do you think we could do as a family so this same thing doesn't happen again?" After the child who raised the issue has given his or her best idea on how to fix the situation, you may say, "Let's see if anyone else has ideas that could work, and then we'll decide as a group which to implement. After all, we all must be able to support it to make the solution work well. It can't just be something that makes one person happy, wouldn't you all agree?"

You would then ask the other family members for their ideas, perhaps listing those on a small whiteboard. After you brainstorm possible solutions, select the one you all agree would be best to try first. Decide how long you should try it out before evaluating it at a future family meeting—remembering that in some cases a good trial period might need to be a matter of weeks, not just one. When you do reevaluate it, if it is not working well for the majority of the group, select a different solution from the original solution list. Also decide at what future meeting to evaluate it. (By the way, it's a good idea to keep a notebook of informal minutes with such decisions listed so that anyone can refer to it at any time).

For the next meeting topic, each person should commit to doing something that week that will help the family and keep things positive—or try to correct a problem identified in the meeting. Each person should also discuss his or her schedule for the week. This would include meetings, appointments, tests, special events, or projects that each child and parent has going on. This way, you can identify any scheduling conflicts or tasks that other family members may need to take on for another.

It's important to remember that the family meeting is going to be most effective if both you and your partner—as the parents—remain committed to it. Also, because everyone is likely finding things tough, allow the children to bring up things that their PTSD-suffering parent may have done that proved upsetting. They should be taught how to do this in a modified three-part assertion where they state "When Dad did such and such" or "When Mom did such and such." The child would then continue on and state his or her emotional response as well as the reason for it. For example, one of the children could complain that Dad, who has recently returned from war, wouldn't let them go and play with their friends in the neighborhood as you've always allowed them to do. This child may say, "When Dad wouldn't let me go play touch football with the neighborhood kids in the park, I felt angry because you've always let us do this, Mom, and nothing has ever happened." The other children may chime in and agree this is a problem for them as well.

When something like this happens, you may tell the children that you and your partner, as the parents, will discuss this alone. However, you should assure the children that by the next family meeting, you'll have an answer regarding this issue. Before you begin talking about the issue the following week, you may want to start off by talking about how their Dad has become overly cautious because of his PTSD. Or, if Dad is at the meeting, perhaps you can get him to mention this himself? You may then want to present some new family rules, or come up with a compromise that keeps the kids happy while also helping Dad remain comfortable while he yet strives to get his PTSD symptoms under better control. You must decide what works for your family—and that certainly includes your partner with PTSD.

It may turn out that your partner is not capable of participating in a family meeting—that more problems are created rather than solved by taking this approach. If this is the case, let your partner off the hook, but still plan to have these weekly meetings with your children. And always remember to model good communication skills and problem solving. By doing so, your children will come to learn these valuable skills as well.

Also, realize that these meetings should be about having fun as a family, too. Set aside some of the time to tell stories or play games. Use these meetings as a means to rebuild a connection as a family that has likely been harmed by PTSD's appearance.

Unfortunately, sometimes all the solutions that you and the children generate are not going to be enough to keep a healthy environment in your PTSD-impacted home. Despite all the new things you have learned here and put into practice, you may discover that it is not possible to develop anything that even resembles a healthy relationship with your partner—and that the promise of ever doing so looks very slim indeed.

Chapter 12

Should You Stay?

244 Your Relationship Bank Account

245 Guiding Beliefs

246 The Chronically Abusive Partner

248 Staying Because of Denial

251 Finding a Solution

Are you in that painful place where you're trying to determine whether your relationship is worth saving? If you're with someone new, it may be less difficult to decide that PTSD brings forth more challenges than you're willing to take on—especially if the individual isn't making a real attempt to get help. But if you've been with your partner for a while—especially if you're married and have a family—this could be a more difficult decision.

While there are undoubtedly various questions going through your mind, the question you may want to think about first is this: What has PTSD brought into your relationship that you're having a particularly difficult time dealing with—or feel that you no longer wish to deal with at all? Is it the fact that your partner is irritated constantly and you struggle with the outbursts of anger? Is it the fact that he won't get help, uses drugs, and is on a destructive path you don't want to walk with him? Maybe you're concerned about how PTSD-induced behaviors affect the children, and you've decided that if your partner won't get help within a certain time frame, you don't want the kids exposed to his behaviors because of potential long-term repercussions. Maybe your partner is seeing another person because he wants to be with someone whose eyes don't tell him that he's changed—and not for the better. You don't want to be a part of this scenario.

You're undoubtedly coping with difficult times, and you may feel alone as you ponder what the future may bring—and what you want to do about it. It may help you to realize that others in your situation have faced similar thoughts. It may also help to read their suggestions for days, weeks, and months like these. These suggestions include:

- You may fear that he'll never be the man you knew before. Try to remember that he has the same fear.
- No matter what she does, adhere to your own moral code. Don't try to retaliate for the pain she or the PTSD may have caused you to suffer. Take the high road instead.
- Remind yourself that, as much as you'd wish it otherwise, you can only do so much for him. He must take actions toward healing and recovery.
- You may have to set firm boundaries. You may have to tell her that either she gets help or you're going to be forced to leave.
- Build a support network because, whether you stay or leave, you can't expect to get through this alone.
- You may feel as if you're going crazy. On days like these, check in with others. Let them remind you that while you're not crazy, the situations you face can be crazy-making.
- If you and your loved one do end up splitting, don't immediately turn to another relationship to help you feel better. Take some time to heal from this one first.
- If you've been reading about how to cope better with a PTSD-impacted relationship but not actually putting any of the recommendations into action, take one of these things and start doing it. Then, after that has become a habit for you, take another action step. In time, you should notice that you—and your relationship—are changing.
- Remember that romantic love is easy because it's practically automatic. However, real love demands that you continually make a choice to be loving. When your loved one has PTSD, time and again you must choose

to be loving despite the obstacles that PTSD hurls your way.

- The person you loved before may still be in there, waiting to re-emerge after PTSD treatment. Then again, you must realize that no matter how committed she is to her recovery or how hard she works on her treatment plan, this may not happen. Are you prepared to deal with this on your own, or could you benefit from professional help?

- Did you know that sometimes the man who has returned from a war zone will do things to get a reaction from you so he can feel the rush of adrenaline again? He may go to a chat room and flirt online—as a tactic to get you upset. But that doesn't mean he's actually having an affair—or intending to do so, either.

- He may not be having an affair, but he may be looking for someone who will accept him and all his self-destructive behaviors. Someone he thinks won't push him to change. If this happens, don't be too harsh on yourself for not wanting to walk beside him on that downward path. But if you do decide to leave, do so graciously. If you have children, it will make things much more pleasant for everyone. You'll also be setting things up to be emotionally healthier for the kids in the future.

- Are you trying to forgive her for all her bad behaviors stemming from the PTSD, but can't seem to do that? You may want to keep reading about PTSD and make a point to chat with others on Internet forums who've been through this. This way, you may gain a level of compassion that will make all of this a little easier for you.

- Is your PTSD-suffering veteran pushing you away? Perhaps he has experienced all the loss he thinks he can handle. He doesn't want to allow himself to be close to anyone again. Of course, he may not voice this sentiment to you because he's likely doing it unconsciously.

- If she elects to leave you, she may be doing it because she thinks she's unworthy of you—and your love. She may also believe she's saving you from the damaged person she has become.

- Remember, your PTSD-suffering spouse might be numb. This means he feels essentially nothing. He's not just rejecting you. He is rejecting everything—you, himself, and life.

- Have you been acting hurt and responding to your partner and his actions out of emotion? If so, try to slow down and not react so quickly. If you'll strive to become more logical, he may respond better.

- Remember, change is never easy and, with PTSD, it can be even more difficult. If your partner has complex PTSD that stems from being in a war zone, it's going to be more difficult yet. But when you're aware of the challenges you face and you become realistic about them, it's often easier to meet them head-on. While you may suspect otherwise, you're actually harmed by remaining ignorant of the truth.

- Stop making your partner your project for change and instead work on changing yourself. When you begin to do this, he'll be forced to change in some way. Also, by focusing on yourself instead of him, you give him the space he may need to begin to make changes. Before, if he felt that you were pushing him, he may have pushed back to keep from being controlled. Once he doesn't have to worry about that, he may feel comfortable stepping forward and making changes on his own.

- Take care of yourself first and your loved one with PTSD second. This way, you'll ensure that you have the good health and energy needed to help him take on his PTSD so he'll become its conqueror.
- Try to add some joy and laughter to each day.
- Remember that many veterans had to engage in black-and-white thinking in the war zone because that could have meant the difference between survival and death in combat. However, this is now destructive for your family. Figure out how you can most gently remind him of this fact—for your sake as well as that of the children.

Has this list inspired your own thought processes? Hopefully, it has. If not, try the following exercise.

EXERCISE DETERMINING CONCERNS ABOUT YOUR RELATIONSHIP

List those things that concern you about your relationship. Then look at each point carefully. Is it a rational or reasonable concern? If it is, put a check mark beside it. Next, look at each point that you checked and ask yourself if it's a deal-breaker or something that suggests that you've been getting too fearful about the future prematurely—perhaps overreacting? Are you painting a picture of darkness when there are rays of hope you've been ➤

failing to acknowledge? Could you be seeking sudden and massive change on your partner's part when she is only capable of taking small steps to tackle her PTSD? If you decide a particular point is a deal-breaker, put another check mark beside it on your list. Then take note of how many deal-breakers there are as opposed to the concerns that are more about fear or other emotions. If the majority of your points are deal-breakers, you may want to seriously start thinking about leaving. But if most fall into the latter group, read on.

You may want to go back and review some of the things that you've learned about changing your thoughts. Are there new techniques that could help you tolerate the situation better—assuming that you really do want to stand by your partner's side? Do you just need to find ways to better cope until the times grow better?

You may also want to write down some of the reasons you began a relationship with your partner in the first place. This may be difficult because many of us are attracted to a certain type of romantic partner for both conscious and unconscious reasons, but you may still be able to make a mental list of the characteristics you wanted in your partner. Maybe you needed your loved one to be fun and someone who embraced life. Maybe you wanted your partner to have a great sense of humor and to be easygoing. Maybe you asked for someone affectionate and loving. And, while the person who's your partner may initially have been all of these things, the PTSD has likely taken many of these traits away—at least for now. You may feel as though you've been left to live with a stranger, but if you write some of these characteristics down—and ➤

if your partner is seeking help for the PTSD—perhaps it will be easier for you to imagine her becoming this way once again. ■

Your Relationship Bank Account

You went into this relationship expecting a partnership, didn't you? You started out with a relationship bank account into which you both made deposits. Likely, you also both made a similar number of withdrawals of nearly equal size. Sure, from time to time one person might have withdrawn more while the other diligently kept making those deposits, but this temporary imbalance was acceptable because you saw it as temporary. You could accept that your partner was going through tough times because of emotional or physical health reasons, for example, and would need to take more from that bank account than he put back in. You also probably suspected that if you ever experienced a time of need, your partner would be there for you as well. Then PTSD entered the picture; now everything has changed.

Perhaps you now feel as though you're making all the deposits. You probably don't see any end to this in sight, either.

If your partner is explosive and abusive because of the combination of PTSD symptoms and any chemical substances he has been using to self-medicate, you may be at your wit's end. If a part of you feels that your relationship is going nowhere but downhill, you may also be telling yourself that it's best to get out sooner than later. However, when you think such thoughts, you may feel consumed by guilt.

Your loved one didn't ask for the PTSD, you remind yourself. This mental disorder is the culprit, while your partner is its unfortunate victim. Furthermore, how can you act like merely a fair-weather friend? If you're married, you may also be trying to remind yourself that you vowed to stand by your partner in sickness and in health.

You suddenly realize that your current way of thinking is keeping you stuck when you have some important decisions to make. How should you be thinking now so you can move forward instead?

Guiding Beliefs

Beliefs drive your behavior, and by now you should realize that you have a choice as to what these beliefs are going to be. You can continue to hold steadfast to the beliefs that you've allowed to direct your life thus far, or you can decide to change those beliefs, allowing you to go forth and behave in different ways than you did previously. You may decide that since your partner is not upholding her end of the bargain, as suggested by her refusal to get treatment, you don't have to stay around and be an abused caregiver. You may decide—or even come to believe—that you were put on this earth to do more than this. Perhaps you'll come to believe that you've gone through this experience so you could realize that people handle misfortune differently. You may now come to feel strongly that you'd prefer to dedicate your time, energy, and talents to others who want to take action and change themselves and their lives, instead of allowing yourself to enable someone who's walking a path toward self-destruction.

You have some tough choices to make. Many times people fail to stop and evaluate changed circumstances and consider what these may ask of them. What are the lessons to be learned in the moment? Are you allowing the part of you that seeks out what is best for you as well as for others to sit in the driver's seat? It's important to remember that if you're starting to feel that things are growing increasingly unsafe, and you need to leave the relationship to remain safe, it may be time to go. While making the decision to leave your partner when she's down and out may seem like a cruel-hearted thing to do, perhaps you're being quietly guided to take this action because it will benefit both of you. Remember, it may be easy for your partner to sit back and do nothing because you're there to be her caregiver. But if you get up and walk away, you may be providing the impetus that your partner needs to take a step toward treatment and health.

If you sense that you're being nudged to move on, but your current beliefs are keeping you stuck, maybe it's time to re-evaluate your beliefs. It's sometimes easy to become the martyr. Actually, the ego seems to take some pleasure in playing that role. But that's not a healthy way to live.

The Chronically Abusive Partner

If you were dealing with a partner who had been abusive toward you for years because he had a personality disorder and abused substances, it might be easier to step back, accept that things weren't likely to get any better, and decide to leave. Because the outcome of such a relationship is almost certain, you would get plenty of encouragement to do so. But the response is not so adamant when it comes to whether you should stay or leave a partner who is currently exhibiting abusive behavior due to PTSD.

You probably want to hold out hope that this unwelcome guest in your relationship won't stay forever. It's important to have such hope—if there's reason for that hope to exist. But if your partner has steadfastly refused to do anything to tackle this problem for some time now, you may be living a life where your relationship bank account just continues to become depleted.

You may also need to be concerned for your safety, and your children's as well. Remember, men suffering from PTSD, especially if they've been trained to be killers in a war zone and have fulfilled that role, may come home and kill a partner or family member. As sad as this is, it has happened and you must face up to this reality. Of course, that's why the need for having a safety plan was covered earlier.

But again, just like you, I want to hold out hope. I elected to write this book because I know that PTSD, addictions, and abuse can often go together in the same way that narcissism, addictions, and abuse can—as I discuss at my website, *www.narcissismaddictionsabuse.com*. Still, I believe that if your PTSD-suffering partner gets help and learns how to better manage his PTSD symptoms, the two of you can carve out a decent future together. And frankly, I hold out more hope for you gaining some happiness in the future with your partner than I do for the partner of the addicted and abusive narcissist—someone unlikely to seek help and change. Of course, this doesn't help you answer the question that may be swirling through your mind these days: Should I stay or should I leave?

It would be nice to be able to tell you what to do, but I certainly don't know what you face—nor can I predict what tomorrow will be like for you, either. So, if you're in a quandary as to whether to stay in your PTSD relationship or to leave, you need to seek good professional help—a therapist who can help you with your decision-making. You may want to consider seeking guidance from a therapist familiar with your partner's case. If your partner's therapist refuses to see you and instead you must find someone for yourself, don't seek out a plain vanilla marital therapist—for example, someone used to simply helping couples who are struggling to re-establish intimacy after hectic schedules pushed them apart. After all, the issues you face are much different. Therefore, seek out someone used to dealing with people facing PTSD, addictions, and abuse issues in a partner.

The therapist may recommend that you stand by your partner while he seeks out needed help—and this therapist may also agree to stand by you as you go through undoubtedly emotionally draining and perhaps harrowing times while your partner seeks to put PTSD behind him. However, the therapist also could suggest that it's unsafe to stay, or that you should be prepared for the fact that what you face today may be easier than what you'll face tomorrow.

Staying Because of Denial

Maybe you're inclined to stay despite myriad problems. Could you be in denial about what's truly happening? If this is the situation, let's review the abuse you're facing—or may have to contend with if the PTSD and your partner's abuse of substances moves forward unchecked.

Physical Abuse

Let's begin by discussing physical abuse. You may think that this is where a man beats a woman up so badly that she lands in the emergency room of the local hospital. But in reality, men as well as women can be victims of physical abuse, and there are other things categorized as physical abuse that aren't this extreme. For example, would you think of physical threats of violence as physical abuse? Perhaps not, but you should. You should also consider the following as physical abuse:

- Pushing
- Shoving
- Hitting
- Slapping
- Punching
- Biting
- Kicking
- Being held down
- Being pinned against the wall
- Having objects thrown at you, or being present while they are thrown in the same room
- Watching your partner break things
- Observing your partner punch the wall or a door
- Having your partner drive recklessly to scare you
- Having your partner block the exit so you can't get away
- Having your partner flash weapons at you

So, now that you realize the types of behaviors that fall into this category, ask yourself if your partner has engaged in any of them since developing PTSD. Have you ignored or minimized the importance of any of these actions?

Verbal and Emotional Abuse

Because of shows like *Oprah* and *Dr. Phil,* more women today are aware of verbal and emotional abuse than were previously. There are also some great books out there that cover these topics. A couple of my favorites were written by Patricia Evans—they seem to particularly open the eyes of women in denial about the extent of verbal abuse in their relationships. You may want to check out *The Verbally Abusive Relationship* and *Verbal Abuse Survivors Speak Out.*

Read these two books or some of the others out there, and you'll discover that more things probably fall under verbal abuse and emotional abuse than you previously imagined. These behaviors include the following:

- Name calling
- Coercion and threats
- Criticizing
- Yelling
- Humiliating a person
- Isolating the person from family and friends
- Controlling finances as well as preventing the person from working
- Threatening to hurt children or pets
- Stalking

The thing is, while your partner may be engaging in some of these behaviors because of PTSD or the use of alcohol to self-medicate, this doesn't make this verbal abuse any less painful or emotionally harmful. Just as the physical violence stemming from your partner's PTSD could still put you in the hospital, the verbal and emotional abuse can destroy your sense of self. Your partner is likely to undermine your very being by attacking those abilities in which you take pride and that also bring you joy. That is also why you may feel that your spirit and soul are withering.

Was There Abuse Before?

Think about your relationship before PTSD entered the picture. Did your partner engage in abuse before PTSD? If he didn't, things will probably get better as your loved one undergoes treatment for PTSD—assuming he is undergoing such treatment and taking it seriously. In this case, you may be in a relationship worth trying to save. But if your partner was engaging in such behaviors before, and the PTSD has only made matters worse, you may want to consider packing your bags.

Finding a Solution

Are you still in a quandary as to whether you should stay or leave? If your partner hasn't had enough time to face up to the fact that she has PTSD, perhaps it's right that you're hanging in there for the time being. Right now, it may be unreasonable to expect your loved one to be taking significant action to change. In fact, both of you may be at one of the first steps in the change process, where you need to gather more information about what you face. As a result, you should be prepared to give your partner more time.

But you may want to consider putting some type of a time limit on how long you'll stick around and watch if your partner essentially does nothing to take on the PTSD. Setting a time limit can help both of you. Why do I say this? Maybe you've been putting pressure on yourself to make a decision one way or the other—to stay or to leave. Rather than doing this to yourself and suffering the resulting anguish, it may work better to decide that you're not going to worry about making this decision for a given amount of time—that is, assuming you're not in grave danger.

Go ahead and implement some of the actions we've talked about so you can better cope with the slings and arrows that you may be forced to endure in your PTSD-infested world. Learn to control yourself and not react to your partner's actions. Remind yourself that you want to do everything you can to maintain calmness in this environment, to help keep both your and your partner's stress levels down. Brush up on your communication skills to help achieve this end. Also, expect the best but be prepared for the worst.

Let me say in closing that I'm going to sit here and imagine things going well for the two of you. I'm anticipating that you'll both begin to take the right actions soon to start tackling the PTSD. I'm also going to let myself imagine that one day, both you and your partner will look back and realize how the two of you grew both as individuals and as a couple because you had to stand up and successfully combat the potential tyranny of PTSD.

Can you also imagine such things for you, your partner, and your relationship? Hopefully so. And toward that end, here's wishing you the best both now and in the future!

Afterword
Seeking Stories

As the partner of someone with PTSD, you're becoming an expert in this disorder and how it impacts the sufferer and others in relationships with him or her. There's also a good chance that others can learn from your experiences. Since many veterans of the Afghanistan and Iraq wars will come to be diagnosed with PTSD—if they haven't been already—what you have learned could prove valuable to them. Therefore, if you have a story or helpful hints to share—and would be open to seeing these appear in a book in the future—please go to *www.PTSDRelationship.com*. There you will find more information about what to submit and how to do so. Generally, Dr. England hopes to hear not only about the struggles you and your partner have faced, but the actions that one or both of you took that proved helpful, or services you came across that were particularly useful. These need not have been huge or momentous things, but they should have brought some relief to the PTSD sufferer or others in the family coping with the changes this disorder can bring to the family system.

Dr. England would like to thank you now for seeking to help others who might follow in your footsteps in this way.

Bibliography

American Psychiatric Association. *Diagnostic and Statistical Manual of Mental Disorders, Fourth Edition.* Washington, D.C.: American Psychiatric Association, 1994.

Armstrong, Keith, Suzanne Best, and Paula Domenici. *Courage after Fire.* Berkeley: Ulysses Press, 2006.

Beck, Aaron. *Cognitive Therapy and the Emotional Disorders.* New York: The New American Library, Inc., 1976.

Beck, Aaron. *Love Is Never Enough.* New York: Harper & Row, 1988.

Bennice, J. A., et al. "The Relative Effects of Intimate Partner Physical and Sexual Violence on Posttraumatic Stress Disorder Symptomalogy." *Violence and Victims*, vol. 18, no. 1 (2003), pp. 87–94.

Board of Veterans Appeals. "How Do I Appeal?" Access: *www.va.gov/vbs/bva.*

Bower, Bruce. "Damage Control: Brain Injuries Fight Off PTSD in Vets." *Science News*, vol. 173, no. 1 (2008), p. 5.

Bradshaw, John. *Healing the Shame That Binds You.* Deerfield Beach, Florida: Health Communications, 1988.

Breed, Allen, and Kevin Maurer. "Hero Couldn't Defeat the Enemy Inside." *Dallas Morning News*, July 21, 2008.

Briere, John. "Therapy for War-Related Trauma." Access video: *www.youtube.com.*

Burns, David. *Feeling Good.* New York: Penguin Group, 1980.

Burns, David. *The Feeling Good Handbook.* New York: Plume, 1989.

Cameron, Julia. *The Artist's Way: A Spiritual Path to Higher Creativity.* New York: Jeremy P. Tarcher/Putnam, 2002.

Carnes, Patrick. *The Betrayal Bond.* Deerfield Beach, Florida: Health Communications, Inc., 1997.

Coming Home Project. "Coming Home Movies." Access videos: *www.cominghomeproject.net.*

Defense Finance and Accounting Service. *Wounded Warrior Entitlements Handbook.* Washington D.C.: Defense Finance and Accounting Service, 2007.

DeFoore, William. *Anger: Deal with It, Heal with It, Stop It from Killing You.* Deerfield, Florida: Heath Communications, 2004.

Deschner, Jeanne. *How to End the Hitting Habit.* New York: The Free Press, 1984.

Doby, Kathy. "Death in the Corps." *Nation,* February 18, 2008.

Dominquez, R., C. F. Nelke, and B. D. Perry. "Child Sexual Abuse," in *Crime and Punishment,* Vol. 1. Thousand Oaks, California: Sage Publications, 2002.

Dutra, Lisa. "Core Schemas and Suicidality in a Chronically Traumatized Population." *Journal of Nervous and Mental Disorders,* vol. 196, no. 1 (2008), pp. 71–74.

Ellis, Albert. *Anger: How to Live With and Without It.* Secaucus, New Jersey: Citadel Press, 1977.

Ellis, Albert, and Robert Harper. *A New Guide to Rational Living.* North Hollywood, California: Wilshire Book Company, 1975.

Evans, Patricia. *Verbal Abuse Survivors Speak Out.* Avon, Massachusetts: Adams Media Corporation, 1993.

Evans, Patricia. *The Verbally Abusive Relationship.* Holbrook, Massachusetts: Adams Publishing, 1992.

Federal Register. "Department of Veteran Affairs: Accreditation of Agents and Attorneys; Agent and Attorney Fees; and Final Rule." *Federal Register,* vol. 73, no. 100 (May 22, 2008), pp. 29852–29880. Access: *www.va.gov/ogc/docs/73FR29850.pdf.*

Fisher, Roger, and William Ury. *Getting to Yes: Negotiating Agreement Without Giving In.* New York: Penguin Books, 1991.

Foa, Edna, Elizabeth Henbree, and Barbara Rothbaum. *Prolonged Exposure Therapy for PTSD.* New York: Oxford University Press, 2007.

Fountain, Kristen. "Examining Assault: Software Provides Virtual Forensic Clinic." *Valley News,* April 14, 2008.

Friedman, Matthew. "Neurobiology and Pharmacotherapy for PTSD." National Center for PTSD. Access: *www.ncptsd.va.gov/ptsd101/modules/Friedman%20Pharm%20Transcript.pdf.*

Friends in Recovery. *The Twelve Steps: A Way Out.* San Diego: RPI Publishing, Inc., 1987.

Frontline PBS. "The Soldier's Heart." Access: *www.pbs.org/wgbh/pages/frontline/shows/heart/view.*

Gilbert, Paul. *Human Nature and Suffering*. New York: The Guilford Press, 1992.

Gottman, John. *A Couple's Guide to Communication*. Champaign, Illinois: Research Press, 1976.

Gottman, John. *The Seven Principles for Making Marriage Work*. New York: Three River Press, 1999.

Gottman, John. *Why Marriages Succeed and Fail*. New York: Firestone Books, 1994.

Grossman, David. *On Killing: The Psychological Cost of Learning to Kill in War and Society*. New York: Back Bay Books, 1996.

Halpern, Sue. "Virtual Iraq." *New Yorker*, May 19, 2008.

Hamblen, Jessica. "What Is PTSD?" National Center for PTSD. Access: *www.ncptsd.va.gov*.

Hedges, Chris. *War Is a Force That Gives Us Meaning*. New York: Anchor Books, 2002.

Hendrix, Harville. *Getting the Love You Want*. New York: Harper Perennial, 1988.

Herman, Judith. *Trauma and Recovery*. New York: Basic Books, 1992.

Huff, Jeanne. "Yoga Nidra: Pretzel-Free Relaxation." *Idaho Statesman*, January 12, 2008.

Johnson, Vernon. *I'll Quit Tomorrow*. San Francisco: Harper & Row Publishers, 1980.

Kasl, Charlotte. *Women, Sex, and Addiction*. New York: Harper & Row Publishers, Inc., 1989.

Kiley, Dan. *Living Together, Feeling Alone*. New York: Prentice Hall Press, 1989.

Kors, Joshua. "Specialist Town Takes His Case to Washington." *Nation*, October 15, 2007.

Kovach, Gretel. "Combat's Inner Cost." *Newsweek*, November 5, 2007.

Lauterbach, Dean, et al. "Quality of Parental Relationships among Persons with a Lifetime History of Posttraumatic Stress Disorder." *Journal of Traumatic Stress*, vol. 20, no. 2 (2007), pp.161–172.

Lindlaw, Scott. "Killing by Drones Stresses Pilots in California." *Valley News*, August 8, 2008.

Lindley, Stephen. "Pharmacological Treatment of PTSD." National Center for PTSD. Access: *www.ncptsd.va.gov/ncmain/ncdocs/videos/emv_psychopharm_mhcp.html*.

Lunney, Carole, and Paula Schnurr. "Domains of Quality of Life and Symptoms in Male Veterans Treated for Posttraumatic Stress Disorder." *Journal of Traumatic Stress*, vol. 20, no. 6 (2007), pp. 955–964.

Maslow, Abraham. *The Farther Reaches of Human Nature*. New York: The Viking Press, Inc., 1971.

Mayo Clinic. "Selective Serotonin Reuptake Inhibitors (SSRIs)." Access: *www.mayoclinic.com/health/ssris/MH00066*.

McFall, Miles. "Multidimensional Assessment of Anger in Vietnam Veterans with Posttraumatic Stress Disorder." *Comprehensive Psychiatry*, vol. 40, no. 3 (1999), pp. 216–220.

McFall, Miles, et al. "Combat-Related Posttraumatic Stress Disorder and Severity of Substance Abuse in Vietnam Veterans." *Journal on Studies of Alcohol*, vol. 53, no. 4 (1992), pp. 357–363.

Miller, Jennifer. "Two Different Wars, One Common Bond." *Christian Science Monitor*, January 30, 2008.

Banasr, Mounira, et al. "Serotonin-Induced Increases in Adult Cell Proliferation and Neurogenesis Are Mediated Through Different and Common 5-HT Receptor Subtypes in the Dentate Gyrus and the Subventricular Zone." *Neuropsychopharmacology*, vol. 29, no. 3 (2004) pp. 450–460.

Najavits, Lisa. *Seeking Safety: A Treatment Manual for PTSD and Substance Abuse*. New York: Guilford Press, 2001.

Najavits, Lisa. "Seeking Safety: An Evidence-Based Model for Substance Abuse and Trauma/PTSD," in *A Therapist's Guide to Evidence-Based Relapse Prevention Therapy*. San Diego: Elsevier Press, 2007.

Najavits, Lisa. "Implementing Seeking Safety Therapy for PTSD and Substance Abuse: Clinical Guidelines." Access: *www.bhrm .org/guidelines/PTSD.pdf*.

National Center for PTSD. "The Iraq War Clinician Guide, Second Edition." Access: *www.ncptsd.va.gov*.

National Center for PTSD. "Partners of Veterans with PTSD: Caregiver Burden and Related Problems." Access: *www.ncptsd .va.gov*.

National Center for PTSD. "Returning from the War Zone: A Guide for Families of Military Personnel." Access: *www.ncptsd .va.gov*.

National Institutes of Health. "Past Child Abuse Plus Variations in Genes Result in Potent PTSD Risk for Adults." Access: *www.nih.gov/news/health/mar2008.*

Naval Inspector General. "Administrative Separation." Access: *www.ig.navy.mil/Complaints/Complaints%20%20(Admin%20 Separations).htm.*

Niehoff, Debra. *The Biology of Violence.* New York: The Free Press, 1999.

NOW/PBS. "Military Sexual Trauma." Access: *www.pbs.org/now/ shows/336/video.html.*

NOW/PBS. "Rape in the Military." Access: *www.pbs.org/now/ shows/421/video-seg1.html.*

Oquendo, Maria, et al. "Association of Comorbid Posttraumatic Stress Disorder and Major Depression with Greater Risk for Suicidal Behavior." *American Journal of Psychiatry*, vol. 160, no. 3 (2003), pp. 580–582.

Peck, Scott. *The Road Less Traveled.* New York: Touchstone Books, 1978.

Pine, Art. "The Elusive Seamless Transition." U.S. Naval Institute *Proceedings* magazine, vol. 134, no. 2 (2008), pp. 44–51. Access: *www.usni.org.*

Prochaska, James, John Norcross, and Carl Diclemente. *Changing for Good.* New York: Morrow and Company, Inc., 1994.

PTSD Forum: Post-Traumatic Stress Disorder Community. Access: *www.ptsdforum.org.*

Rand National Defense Research Institute. *An Analysis of Military Disability Compensation.* Santa Monica, California: 2005.

Raskind, Murray, et al. "A Parallel Group Placebo Controlled Study of Prazosin for Trauma Nightmares and Sleep Disturbance in Combat Veterans with Posttraumatic Stress Disorder." *Biological Psychiatry*, volume 61, no. 8, (2007), pp. p 417-420.

Rico, Gabriele. *Pain and Possibility: Writing Your Way Through Personal Crisis*. Los Angeles: Jeremy P. Tarcher, Inc., 1991.

Rizzo, Albert. "Virtual Iraq Therapy for PTSD Sufferers." Access: *www.youtube.com*.

Robinson, Julie. "Vets Taking PTSD Drugs Die in Sleep." *Charleston Gazette*, May 28, 2008.

Roche, John. *The Veteran's Survival Guide: How to File and Collect on VA Claims*. Dulles, Virginia: Potomac Books, Inc., 2007.

Rosellini, Gayle, and Mark Worden. *Taming Your Turbulent Past*. Pompano Beach, Florida: Health Communications, 1987.

Samelius, Charlotta, et al. "Somatization in Abused Women." *Journal of Women's Health*, vol. 16, no. 6 (2007), pp. 909–918.

Schnurr, Paula. "The Rocks and Hard Places in Psychotherapy Outcome Research." *Journal of Traumatic Stress*, vol. 20, no. 5 (2007), pp. 779–792.

Schnurr, Paula. "Cognitive Behavioral Therapy for Posttraumatic Stress Disorder in Women." *Journal of the American Medical Association*, vol. 29, no. 8 (2007), pp. 820–830.

Schottenbauer, Michele, et al. "Contributions of Psychodynamic Approaches to Treatment of PTSD and Trauma: A Review of the Empirical Treatment and Psychopathology Literature." *Psychiatry*, vol. 71, no. 1 (2008), pp. 13–34.

Seligman, Martin. *Authentic Happiness*. New York: Free Press, 2002.

Shay, Jonathan. "About Medications for Combat PTSD." Sidran Institute website. Access: *www.sidran.org/sub .cfm?contentID=50&sectionid=4.*

Shay, Jonathan. *Achilles in Vietnam: Combat Trauma and the Undoing of Character*. New York: Scribner, 2003.

Sherman, Michelle, Dona Zanotti, and Dan Jones. "Key Elements in Couples Therapy with Veterans with Combat-Related Posttraumatic Stress Disorder." *Professional Psychology Research and Practice*, vol. 6, no. 3 (2005), pp. 626–633.

Sontag, Deborah, and Amy O'Leary. "Dr. Jonathan Shay on Returning Veterans and Combat Trauma." *New York Times* Audio Interview. Access: *www.nytimes.com/2008/01/13.*

Spiegel, Alix. "Soldiers' Head Injuries May Contribute to PTSD." NPR's *All Things Considered*, January 31, 2008. Access: *www.npr .org/templates/story/story.php?storyId=18550948.*

Stone, Andrea. "Mental Toll of War Hitting Female Service Members." *USA Today*, January 2, 2008.

Substance Abuse and Mental Health Services Administration Center for Substance Abuse Prevention: SAMHSA Model Programs. Access: *http://modelprograms.sansha.gov.*

Tick, Edward. *War and the Soul: Healing Our Nation's Veterans from Post-Traumatic Stress Disorder*. Wheaton, Illinois: Quest Books, 2005.

Temple, J. R., et al. "Differing Effects of Partner and Nonpartner Sexual Assault on Women's Mental Health." *Violence Against Women*, vol. 13, no. 3 (2007), pp. 28–97.

Tick, Edward. "Healing PTSD with Ed Tick." Access: *www .youtube.com*.

Tolle, Eckhart. *A New Earth*. New York: Plume, 2005.

Tolle, Eckhart. *The Power of Now*. Novato, California: New World Library, 2004.

Vasterling, Jennifer. "PTSD and Neurocognition." *PTSD Research Quarterly*, vol. 18, no. 1 (2007), pp. 1–3. Access: *www.ncptsd .va.gov*.

Walsh, Froma. "Traumatic Loss and Major Disasters: Strengthening Family and Community Resilience." *Family Process*, vol. 46, no. 2 (2007), pp. 207–227.

Wounded Warrior Project. "DOD/VA Disability Rating System Reform." Access: *www.woundedwarriorproject.org*.

Zoroya, Greg. "A Fifth of Soldiers at PTSD Risk." *USA Today*, March 7, 2008.

Zwerdling, Daniel. "Efforts Build to Help Forgotten Troops with PTSD." NPR's *All Things Considered*, December 20, 2007. Access: *www.npr.org/templates/story/story.php?storyId=17362654*.

Index

Abuse, 246–48
    physical, 248–49
    prior, 251
    sexual, of children, 226–27
    verbal and emotional, 250–51
Acceptance stage of grief, 111–13
Active/reflective listening, 158–62
Addiction, to drugs, 43–44
Adversity, irrational beliefs about, 142–43
Al-Anon, 92–93, 119
Alcoholics Anonymous 12-Step program, 49, 92
Alprozalam, 40–42
American Cancer Society, 191
American Diabetes Association, 126
American Heart Association, 125, 126
American Psychological Association, 76
Anger
    dealing with explosive, 208–10
    as stage of grief, 102–3
    treatment of, 39–40
Anxiety Disorders Association of America, 76, 93
Approval
    irrational beliefs about need for, 138–39
    request for, in art of correction, 165–67

Association for Advancement of Behavioral and Cognitive Therapies, 76
Association of Social Work Boards (ASWB), 73
Ativan, 40
Attitude of gratitude, 131
Avoidance symptoms, 12, 15–18, 22–23

Bargaining stage of grief, 108–10
Behavior
    irrational beliefs about, 143–45, 147–48
    preferred, in art of correction, 165–67
Benzodiazepines, avoiding of, 40–43
Beta-blockers, 40
Brainstorming, for solving problems, 179–80

Caffeine, 42–43
Caregiver role, of child in dysfunctional family, 225–26
Case studies
    active listening, 159–60, 161–62
    anger stage of grief, 103–4
    art of correction, 166–67

Case studies—*continued*
   changing expectations, 128–29
   cognitive restructuring, 60–61
   collecting symptom data,
     24–25
   conflict resolution, 172–73
   contacting therapist, 79–82
   flashbacks, 13–14
   psychodynamic therapy, 94–96
   suicide, 200–204
   talking with children, 218–20
   Vietnam War and children,
     214–15
Celexa, 33
Childhood beliefs, irrationality and,
  148–51
Childhood trauma, 5–6
Children, meeting needs of, 211–36
   defense mechanisms and chil-
     dren, 212–13
   discipline and, 200–236
   dysfunctional family roles,
     221–27
   reassuring of, 227–28
   talking freely with, 217–21
   Vietnam War and, 213–17
Choose to Move program, 125
Cialis, 34–35
Citalopram, 33
Clown role, in dysfunctional family,
  223–24
Cognitive behavioral therapy (CBT),
  51–52
Cognitive processing therapy (CPT),
  64–65
Cognitive restructuring, 57–61

Colleges and universities, therapy
  and, 78
Conflicts, getting at underlying,
  168–73
Cooperative Extension Systems,
  196, 226
Correction, art of, 164–67
Cost cutting, 188–93

Daizepam, 40
Deep breathing, 86–88
Defense, Department of (DOD), 21
Defense mechanisms, of children,
  212–13
Denial stage of grief, 102
Depression
   as stage of grief, 110–11
   therapy and, 49–50
Desyrel, 36
Diet, importance of good, 125–27
Discipline, children and, 230–36
Dysfunctional families, children's
  roles in, 221–27

Ellis, Dr. Albert, 134
Emotional abuse, 250–51
Emotions, irrational beliefs about
  control of, 146
Erectile dysfunction, treatment for,
  34–35
Escitalopram, 33
Exercise, for caregiver, 124–25
Exercises
   analyzing conflict and expecta-
     tions, 174–77

changing problematic thoughts,
58–60
collecting symptom data,
22–24
deep breathing, 87–88
hand-me-down beliefs, 149–51
problem-solving worksheet,
181
stages of grief, 105–7, 109–10
staying in relationship, 242–44
Expanded Food and Nutrition Education Program (EFNEP), 127
Expectations
analyzing of, 173–79
changing of, 128–31
Exposure therapy, 52–55
Eye movement desensitization and
reprocessing (EMDR), 55–58

Fairness, irrational beliefs about,
139–40
Family meetings, 231–36
Family physicians, therapy and, 78
Financial matters, 184–96
budgeting, 185–87
conflicts about, 168–73
cutting costs, 188–93
insurance issues, 193–95
sources of help, 195–96
Flashbacks, 13–15
Fluozetine, 32–33
Foa, Dr. Edna B., 53
Friends, handling lack of support
from, 119–20
Friends in Recovery, 88

Gratitude, having attitude of, 131
Grief, stages of, 99–113
acceptance, 111–13
anger, 102–4
bargaining, 108–10
denial, 102
depression, 110–11
Group formats, 90–93
Guns, household safety and, 209

Halcion, 40–42
Hand-me-down beliefs, irrationality
and, 148–51
Health maintenance organizations,
for therapy information, 78
Help, asking for, 121–22
Hero role, in dysfunctional family,
222–23
Human resource offices, therapist
information in, 77
Hyperarousal symptoms, 12, 18–19,
22–23

Illegal drugs, 43–44
Image rehearsal therapy (IRT), 55–57
Incentive, offering in art of correction, 165–67
Insomnia, treatment of, 35–36
Insurance matters, 193–95
Integrative restoration (iRest), 89–90
iRest, 89–90
Irrational beliefs
about actions and anger,
143–45

Irrational beliefs—*continued*
    about actions and punishment,
        140–41
    about certain needs being met,
        134–35
    about challenges and future,
        142–43
    about childhood versus adult-
        hood, 148–51
    about control of behavior,
        147–48
    about control of emotions, 146
    about determination of worth,
        136–37
    about fair treatment, 139–40
    about handling certain events,
        135–36
    about need for approval, 138–39
    about pleasure versus harm,
        145–46

Kübler-Ross, Dr. Elisabeth, 101

Lawyers Serving Warriors, 21, 22,
    195
Levitra, 34–35
Lexapro, 33
Licensing, of therapy professionals,
    69–70, 72–74
Lindley, Dr. Stephen, 28
Listening
    active or reflective listening,
        158–62
    speaker/listener technique,
        163–64

Lorazepam, 40
Lost child role, in dysfunctional
    family, 227

Marriage and family counselors, 75
Mascot role, in dysfunctional family,
    223–24
Medications, 27–44
    effectiveness/dosage/interac-
        tions, 29–31
    selective serotonin reuptake
        inhibitors, 32–40
    therapy and, 28, 47–48
    those best avoided, 40–43
Meditation, iRest and, 90
Mental health, of caregiver, 127–28
Military sexual trauma (MST), 8–10
Miller, Dr. Richard, 90
Monoamine oxidase inhibitor
    (MAOI), 34
Multiple channel exposure therapy
    (MCET), 63–65

Najavits, Dr. Lisa, 50
National Association of Social
    Workers, 76
National Center for Victims of
    Crime, 77
National Center of American Heart
    Association, 125
Needs, irrational beliefs about, 134–35
Nightmares, treatment of, 35–36,
    55–57

Panic attacks, therapy for, 63–65
Paroxetine, 33
Pastoral counselors, 74–75
Paxil, 33, 36–37
Phone books, locating therapists in, 77
Physical abuse, 248–49
Physical health, of caregiver, 127–28
Pleasure
    finding despite adversity, 135–36
    irrational beliefs about harm and, 145–46
Positive affirmations, 165–67
Post-Traumatic Stress Disorder (PTSD), 2–4
    symptoms of, 12–19
    tracking symptoms of, 19–24
    who gets, 4–12
Prazosin, 35–36
Pregnancy, Paxil and, 36–37
Problem-solving, 179–80
Prolonged Exposure (PE) program, 53–54
Prozac, 32–33
Psychodynamic therapy, 93–96
Psychologists, 73
Punishment, irrational beliefs about, 140–41

Questions, how to ask, 155–56

Rage. See Anger
Re-experiencing symptoms, 12, 13–15, 22–23

Relationship tools, 153–82
    active or reflective listening, 158–62
    art of correction, 164–67
    expectations and, 173–79
    problem-solving, 179–80
    questions to ask, 155–56
    speaker/listener technique, 163–64
    time-outs, 156–58
    underlying conflicts and, 168–73

Safety issues, 19, 209–10
Seeking Safety program, 50–52, 90–91
Selective serotonin reuptake inhibitors (SSRIs), 32–40
Self-care, 115–32
    asking for help, 121–22
    avoiding bad diet, 125–27
    changing expectations, 128–31
    combating stress, 123–25
    finding support, 119–20
    focusing on self, 118–19
    having attitude of gratitude, 131
    need for sleep, 123
    partner's behavior and, 132
    promoting physical and mental health, 127–28
    stepping off victim-rescuer-persecutor triangle, 116–18
Self-help groups, 90–93
Self-protection, 48
Self-worth, irrational beliefs about, 136–37
Serotonin syndrome, 33–34

Sertraline, 33

Sex, avoidance symptoms and, 15–16

Sexual abuse, of child in dysfunctional family, 226–27

Sexual assault survivors, 6–10
therapy for, 62–65

Sexual dysfunction, treatment of, 34–35

Shay, Dr. Jonathan, 10–11, 28, 39

Sleep
for caregiver, 123
insomnia treatment, 35–36
for PTSD sufferer, 96–98

Social workers, 73

Solutions, art of correction and, 165–67

Speaker/listener technique, 163–64

Staying in relationship, decisions about, 237–52
chronic abuse and, 246–51
guiding beliefs and, 245–46
relationship bank account, 244–45

St. John's Wort, 34

Stress, combating of caregiver's, 123–25

Stress inoculation training (SIT), 65

Substance use disorder (SUD), therapy and, 49–52

Suicide, 10, 196–208
conditions associated with increased risk of, 197–98
prevention help, 207–8
SSRIs and, 37–39
talking about, 199–204
warning signs of, 204–7

Support groups, for caregiver, 119–20

Surrogate parent role, of child in dysfunctional family, 225–26

Surrogate spouse role, of child in dysfunctional family, 226–27

Symptoms, of PTSD, 12–19

Therapy options, 45–65
advocating for, 46–48
discussing specific symptoms with therapist, 20
exercise or changing problematic thoughts, 58–60
for PTSD, SUD, and depression, 49–52
for PTSD alone, 52–55
for sexual assault survivor, 62–65

Therapy professionals, 67–83
comfort and trust in, 69–72
family physician and, 78
finding with PTSD experience, 75–78
importance of honesty with, 68–69
kinds of, 72–75
making contact with, 78–85
style of, 71–72

Thinking, changing of. *See* Irrational beliefs

Three-part assertions, 106–7, 165–67

Tick, Dr. Edward, 10–11

Time-outs, 156–58

Triazolam, 40–42

Twelve Steps: A Way Out, The (Friends in Recovery), 88

United States Dept.of Human Services Substance Abuse and Mental Health Services Administration, 76–77

Valium, 40
Verbal Abuse Survivors Speak Out, 250
Verbal and emotional abuse, 250–51
Verbally Abusive Relationship, The, 250
Veterans, 10–12, 17–18
    military sexual trauma and, 8–10
    suicide and, 37–39
    Virtual Iraq therapy program, 54–55
Veterans Affairs, Department of, 21
Viagra, 34–35
Victim-rescuer-persecutor triangle, 116–18
Vietnam war, children and, 213–17
Violence, 19
Virtual Iraq therapy program, 54–55

Walking, as stress-reducing, 124
Writing, help via, 88–89

Xanax, 40–42

Yoga, 89

Zoloft, 33

About the Author

Dr. Diane England, a licensed clinical social worker with other degrees in family studies and child development, has worked with military families overseas in Aviano, Italy, during wartime, and has held positions with the government, national voluntary health organizations, the University of Idaho Cooperative Extension Service, and in private practice. She has spent her career helping individuals strengthen their bodies, their relationships, and their lives. For more information about Diane England, PhD, visit *www.PTSDRelationship.com*.